WHY *the* GOSPEL WITNESSES AGREE

And What This Means for Us

Everett Coates

WHY the GOSPEL WITNESSES AGREE

And What This Means for Us

EVERETT COATES

AMBASSADOR INTERNATIONAL
GREENVILLE, SOUTH CAROLINA & BELFAST, NORTHERN IRELAND

www.ambassador-international.com

WHY THE GOSPEL WITNESSES AGREE
And What This Means for Us

© 2011 Everett Coates

All rights reserved

Printed in the United States of America

ISBN: 978-1-935507-41-3

Cover Design & Page Layout by David Siglin of A&E Media

Scripture quotations taken from the NEW AMERICAN STANDARD BIBLE®,

Copyright © 1960, 1962, 1963, 1968, 1971, 1972, 1973, 1975, 1977, 1995 by The Lockman Foundation

Used by permission. (www.Lockman.org)

AMBASSADOR INTERNATIONAL
Emerald House
427 Wade Hampton Blvd.
Greenville, SC 29609, USA
www.ambassador-international.com

AMBASSADOR BOOKS
The Mount
2 Woodstock Link
Belfast, BT6 8DD, Northern Ireland, UK
www.ambassador-international.com

The colophon is a trademark of Ambassador

Everett Coates has a passion to explain the supposed inconsistencies in the Gospels and to uncover the "lies" of macroevolution. Not only has he reconciled the supposed difficulties, but has done it in a unique, clever opening story concerning the observations of witnesses to a robbery. When Everett asked me to review his writing, I was quickly absorbed in the manner in which he tells a story about witnesses who saw the same event differently. From there Everett carefully analyses the scriptures from the Gospels that relate to various events in the life of Jesus. In all cases he develops justifications for supposed differences in the passages, or what some have called inconsistencies, by showing the interpretation of events as seen through different eyes. I was especially impressed with Everett's high regard for scripture and that he believes it truly represents an accurate historical record of the life and times of Jesus.

I recall having many questions about certain Biblical passages after I began serious scripture reading. Most of the so called inconsistencies I had reconciled in my own mind because I trusted the source (God- breathed) and Jesus' own words in John, telling the disciples that He (Jesus) would send the Holy Spirit and bring to their remembrances all that He had said (John chapters 14, 15, and 16, specifically 14:26). There are also the writings of the Apostle Paul in which he said "All scripture is inspired by God and profitable for teaching, for reproof, for correction, for training in righteousness." 2 Timothy 3:16

My prayer, as I'm certain is Everett's prayer, that Christians who may have doubts or concerns about liberal interpretations of scripture will have their faith strengthened from this book and that skeptics will receive scriptures with respect because of the historical accuracy they contain.

—C. Gerald Van Dyke, PhD

Table of Contents

CHAPTER 1
Witnesses — 9

CHAPTER 2
Why Combine the Gospel Accounts? — 23

CHAPTER 3
The Birth of Jesus — 37

CHAPTER 4
The Crucifixion, Death, and Resurrection of Jesus — 47

CHAPTER 5
The Second Coming of Jesus — 83

CHAPTER 6
What is the Significance? — 89

CHAPTER 7
Consequences — 135

BACK MATTER
Appendix / Works Cited — 152

Chapter 1
Witnesses

"Kyle, get out!" His roommate's shout jerked Kyle out of his drug-induced sleep. The first thing he remembered was Jake's warning to run without question if he ever yelled. Kyle rolled off the couch and stumbled toward the front door. Something was very wrong in the back of the ramshackle farmhouse they were renting. It did not smell the way it usually did when a batch was cooking. Jake had really fouled something up this time!

Kyle heard Jake frantically running down the cluttered hallway, tripping over bags of trash being hoarded inside the house so they would not be found and traced. He was cursing at the top of his lungs as he struggled to get to safety before it was too late. But it was already too late. Kyle twisted the doorknob desperately and flung open the old wooden door to the afternoon sunlight. He had just stepped onto the rickety front porch when the house exploded behind him, throwing him, unconscious, into the weed-choked yard.

Kyle woke up twenty minutes later and sat up, rubbing the singed hair on the back of his head. Where the house had stood was a burning pile of rubble, and lying under the pile somewhere was Jake's mangled body. Kyle Jordan was alone. Again.

That had been two days ago, and now Kyle was rumbling along down Highway 97 just below the posted speed limit toward

Willow Creek, and the lives of four unsuspecting people were about to be turned upside down.

It was a beautiful mid morning in early April with warm sunlight bathing the rural community of Willow Creek in a sepia glow. The hardwood trees were now in full bloom and a fine dusting of pollen had silently blanketed everything that had not moved during the night.

Willow Creek was nothing more than a crossroads, and if not for the four-way stop intersection, drivers passing through wouldn't even slow down to notice. Huddled about the stop signs were several small businesses which served the basic needs of the hundred or so families living within a five-minute drive. There was a hairdresser's shop, a rather run-down "antique store" that sold an odd assortment of old stuff, like a kind of permanent yard sale, and a small hardware store. About a hundred and fifty yards or so from the intersection, well away from "downtown," stood Willow Creek Grocery, a place that everybody simply referred to as "The Store" since it had been there long before most of the others came along. A nesting cardinal serenaded no one in particular as she sat warming her eggs in a lone dogwood tree that stood beside The Store's gravel and dirt parking lot. The building's once-white weatherboard siding needed a fresh coat of paint which it wasn't likely to get for another couple of years. Like most things in this sleepy little community, it could wait. Inside the store, four locals were going about life as always on this quiet, cool morning.

Fred Willis, a local dump truck driver who weighed in at a rather non-athletic two hundred and fifteen pounds, was looking for a candy bar and soft drink to tide him over until lunch. A young housewife named Judy Turner had stopped by on her way home to pick up a gallon of milk. She wanted it to serve cold with the warm oatmeal and raisin cookies that would be waiting for her children when they returned home from school that afternoon. Jim Cassel, a middle-aged, slightly balding snack salesman was restocking his product display and wondering if he ought to ask about moving it to a more visible location in the little store. He came in every other week because for some reason sales in Willow Creek Grocery were slower than the rest of his route. The three smiled and chatted with each other and with Willie Jones, the cashier and owner, as they leisurely went about their business. No one was ever in a hurry.

There was no commercial background music, but the gentle strains of a country ballad from Willie's radio hidden behind the counter served nicely. Fred sang along more than a little off key, but no one really cared. It was okay if things weren't quite perfect. There was no security camera or silent alarm in the store to discourage would-be thieves. None was really needed since there had never been a robbery in the community that anyone could remember. Willow Creek was a peaceful neighborhood, and the world seemed not to have intruded upon it for decades. No doubt, that was mainly because the world and its problems had never really been wanted there. In Willow Creek, change was definitely not good.

However, like it or not, change was coming and life would never quite be the same. The barely muffled sound of the '92 Camaro's rumbling engine preceded it into the parking lot, breaking the reverie of the morning. Calling out her displeasure at having been so rudely disturbed by such noise, the cardinal fluttered across the road into the green-shadowed safety of the woods. The car pulled up parallel to the front of the building, stopped, then backed into an unmarked parking space between Jim's delivery truck and Judy's van. Killing the engine, the driver watched as a small cloud of dust, stirred to life by his car's tires, drifted away in the gentle breeze.

The cooling metal of the dual exhaust pipes ticked an uneven beat as Kyle sat for a moment, not moving, still gripping the steering wheel. As long as he held onto something, his hands would not shake. His eyes darted about invisibly behind dark green sunglasses, taking note of the other vehicles.

Because he held a particular dislike for Willow Creek, he seldom drove through it and never stopped. He had grown up in a similar little country neighborhood in another state and had vowed not to spend time in such places ever again. They reminded him of the painful childhood he had had to survive thanks to his abusive, drug-addicted father. Kyle hadn't even bothered to attend his father's funeral three years ago. Now outwardly all was calm, but inside his mind was racing. He had recently begun to notice that thinking coherently was becoming a chore. Sweat began to trickle down his forehead even though the day was still rather cool.

"Man, what am I doing?" Kyle asked no one.

Gathering courage from odd corners of his mind, Kyle opened the car door. Leaving the keys in the ignition, he unfolded his under-nourished frame and stood looking around silently, almost as if he were hearing the quiet sounds of the country for the first time. He reached into a side pocket in his black leather jacket and pulled out an old knitted toboggan. He frowned nervously, glad that no one could look behind his sunglasses to see the fear in his eyes. Finally, need overcame uncertainty and, pulling on the hat, a gift from his mother whom he still loved but had not seen in two years, he turned toward the door. As he walked he tucked most of his dirty blond hair under the cap. Dirty was not so much a description of color as it was a condition, along with being slightly singed from the explosion. His hand went back into the pocket, this time closing uncomfortably around the grip of a .45 caliber automatic pistol. It was standard equipment for a drug dealer, or so Jake had said. Even so he had never had to use it in the line of duty, so to speak, and had only fired it a couple of times at a paper target tacked to a tree. But this was different. Very different. And Kyle was suddenly very scared.

Kyle's drug addiction was the only inheritance left to him by his father, and he had to get several hundred dollars quickly. Methamphetamine was a commodity that he now had to buy since his friend had been killed when his lab exploded. Jake had been the "chemist" who made the drug, supplying him with it to replace his cocaine habit. Kyle was the salesman always looking for others with whom to share the gift of dependency—for a substantial price, of course.

Their small but growing business had provided more than enough money to buy all the dangerous chemicals needed for the meth production as well as food and other normal life necessities. But when Jake and the house both disappeared in the fireball, Kyle found himself out of income, drugs, food, luck, and everything else. So here he was standing in front of a store he hated, in a community he hated, about to do something he hated having to do. But what he really hated most was the person he had become.

In spite of his fear, hatred, and growing paranoia, a side effect of his meth addiction, Kyle moved toward the door, pulled it open with his non-shooting hand, and stepped inside. His eyes adjusted slowly to the dim light made even dimmer by his sunglasses, which he finally had to raise for a moment to take in his surroundings.

Judy looked at the young man and smiled, noticing his blue eyes that looked a little blood shot and the strand of blond hair trying to escape under the edge of the red toboggan he was wearing. Being a mother, the thought crossed her mind that both the toboggan and the hair could be cleaner. And wasn't the hair slightly burned too? Kyle didn't really care if his unusual appearance drew attention because he was on a mission. Besides, meth addicts generally didn't care how they looked. However, mission or not, he couldn't bring himself to walk directly to the counter. Instead he turned toward the shelves of junk food, not just out of fear but because he hadn't eaten in a day and a half, and picked up something chocolate. Jim, the snack salesman, noticed that the kid looked a bit thin as Kyle picked a small cake and turned quickly. Jim sniffed. There was an odd chemical smell about the boy. Putting the snack in his left pocket, Kyle walked toward the cash register and a smiling, unsuspecting Willie. As he walked he pulled the .45 from his pocket in a shaking right hand and pointed it at Willie's face, which suddenly lost its grin. Being a gun enthusiast himself, Willie noted the gun's make and caliber almost without thinking about it.

"Give me all the money in the register," Kyle said in a rather quiet voice that did not sound nearly as tough as when he had practiced on the way to the store.

"What? Are … are you kidding?" Willie stammered. He somehow knew that the young man was not kidding and that the gun aimed at his forehead was not a joke, but he laughed nervously anyway. Small talk and laughter were sometimes helpful in awkward situations, and this was pretty awkward.

"You heard me," Kyle said, wanting very much to already be out the door and gone. "Get a bag and fill it … now!" Willie swallowed hard and glanced past the gun for help. Perhaps one of his nice customers happened to have a shotgun or something that would be handy just now. Of course, he knew better.

Looking behind him, Kyle saw that he and his gun were now the center of attention and all eyes were on him. He cursed himself for forgetting the customers were there. For some reason he was surprised that no one was moving. Fred had stopped singing but had forgotten to close his mouth. The radio went on without him. Judy gripped her gallon of milk, which was beginning to chill her palms as she held the jug tightly. Jim had instinctively raised his hands as he stood in front of his display rack, vanilla and chocolate cakes squeezed into shapeless masses in iron grips. Taken all together, they looked rather comical, but no one saw the humor. This could not be happening. Not in Willow Creek!

"Everybody on the floor now or I shoot your friendly neighborhood grocer here," Kyle snarled. In an instant they were lying on their faces in front of him. He smiled approvingly as he exerted his newfound power over these complete strangers. "Not you, idiot!" Kyle shouted in spite of himself as he looked back at where the cashier had been standing. Being the compliant sort, Willie had joined his customers on the floor. "Get up and get me the money! I ought to shoot you just for bein' stupid! And hurry!" Letting out a string of profanity and slapping the counter with his open left hand for emphasis, Kyle made it clear that he was not pleased at the extra time this was taking. The sense of power and control was getting to him now, and he was beginning to enjoy his new role of momentary lord of this backwater kingdom. Life and death were his to give or take. But he still wanted more than anything to be gone. Willie struggled to his feet and, forgetting to ask if the young man preferred paper, pulled a plastic bag off the rack and began stuffing bills into it as fast as his shaking hands would allow.

"Please, d-don't shoot me kid—I'm doin' it … I'm doin' it, see?" Willie stammered as he finished cleaning out the cash drawer, all the while wishing he had a gun himself but knowing that he would have been too scared to use it.

"I'm not a kid and I could blow your head off right now!" Kyle nearly screamed, suddenly very impatient. Willie jammed the last of the cash into the bag and put it on the counter, not certain whether it would be his final act. Kyle grabbed the stuffed bag and looked back at his new subjects as they lay on the floor, helpless in his presence and hoping for his favor in not killing them. Taking in the scene, he slowly waved his weapon over them. As if to demonstrate his absolute power, he raised it toward the ceiling and slowly squeezed the trigger. The violence of the gunshot caused everyone in the store to flinch, including Kyle. As plaster and dust showered his toboggan, he suddenly remembered what he was supposed to do next.

"If anybody follows me out the door, you won't live to take a second step!" Kyle threatened. He had heard that line in a movie once and had thought it was cool, so he used it. Recovering his earlier sense of urgency, he bolted out the door into the parking lot, yanked open his car door, and jumped inside. With a twist of the key so forceful it nearly bent in his hand, the engine roared to life. Dust and gravel sprayed the store and parked vehicles as the car fishtailed away from the old building and onto the road, tires squealing. In seconds the car and its fugitive driver were out of sight. Only a cloud of dust and a blue haze of smoke from the burning rubber were left as a fleeting memorial to the car's having been there at all. The twin rubber tire tracks on the pavement left a bold sign for all that read, "He went this way."

Without thinking, and ignoring the final warning, Fred had scrambled to his feet and run to the door to watch the departing car. Black Camaro, early 90s, license number began with the letters ABJ. All he wanted was to help identify this punk and put him behind bars. But he would have to stop shaking first and somehow keep from throwing up. As he stood gazing, his ears still ringing from the gunshot, he watched as the cardinal flew silently back to her nest and inspected her eggs for damage. Seeing none, she settled back into her rightful place as if nothing had changed in the world.

By the time Fred turned back from the door, Willie had already called 911 and was talking with the dispatcher, answering an endless string of questions. Who? What? When? Where? All the usual things. Only after he was assured that a sheriff's deputy would be there in fifteen to twenty minutes did Willie hang up. Somehow just talking to someone associated with law and order, even if the man was miles away on the other end of a telephone line, made him feel better.

"Are you all right?" Fred asked the pale and shaken man as he hung up the phone. Willie nodded that he was and sat down hard on his wooden stool behind the counter. He was not really, but it seemed manlier to pretend to be. He began to feel nauseated as he remembered the sight of the gun aimed at his head, a vision that would wake him from sound sleep for many years to come. "Is everybody okay?" the truck driver added as he looked around the store, remembering there were others there besides himself and Willie. "Ma'am, are you hurt?" he asked as he hurried to where Judy was now sitting on the floor crying uncontrollably.

"No, … I'm … fine," she managed to get out between sobs. "Who was that? Why on earth would anybody want to rob *this* store?" she added, not quite ready to begin regaining her composure. Crying seemed most appropriate at the moment, so she continued.

"I don't know," Jim responded, "but I hope the cops get here soon. I want that guy caught … now!" He realized that, even after hitting the floor on command and standing again, he still had the unrecognizable snack cakes in a death grip. He shook them loose onto the floor.

They occupied themselves with nervous talk about their experience and tried to calm down as they brushed the dust from their clothes. The men hovered over Judy, not really knowing what to do as she gradually stopped crying. The distant sound of sirens began to rise into their consciousness as they talked.

"Well, it's about time," Willie said to the little group. "You'd think the cops could at least try to get to the scene of a crime a little quicker than that."

Only thirty seconds or so behind its siren, the deputy's cruiser slid into the parking lot, followed almost immediately by another, and then another. The cavalry had rather noisily arrived and the robbery victims finally felt secure. Like the Three Stooges plus one, they tried as a group to push through the door and began talking, their words spilling out in a jumble. Having determined the direction of the crook's escape, one deputy took off in pursuit, calling for additional backup.

"It's all right," another deputy said in a soothing voice, holstering his weapon, which he had partially drawn as soon as the door had been thrown open. "Everything will be okay," he said, smiling as he walked toward the agitated four.

"We're going to secure the area now to protect any evidence from being lost. You folks go back inside. The detectives are on their way and will take your statements when they get here." As he ushered them toward the door he added, "Does anybody need medical help?" The four assured him that they were fine and obediently reentered the store. The deputy joined his associate as he rolled out the yellow crime scene tape, draping it around the greater part of the parking lot. By now, of course, the commotion had attracted a small crowd that had to be kept at a distance.

In a few minutes another siren announced the arrival of two detectives who slowly pulled their black, unmarked Crown

Vic cruiser through the knot of curious onlookers into the lot, stopping at the tape line. One of the uniformed officers went into the store and came back out with three of the four eyewitnesses, who were taken to separate cars to sit and relax. One of the detectives then went inside to start the interview process with the fourth.

Standing outside the yellow ribbon, one of the onlookers finally overcame his normal timidity and asked one of the deputies as he stood nearby, "Why are they only talking to one at a time? Wouldn't it be quicker to get all of their information at once? You'll never catch the guy at this rate."

Always patient with those who knew nothing about law enforcement, the deputy replied, "Yes, sir, it would be quicker. But we wouldn't get as much useful information if they were interviewed together." The man's puzzled look led the clean-cut young officer to continue. "If we interview all of the eyewitnesses to a crime separately, each one will remember more details than if they all hear each other's accounts. Each witness may have seen things that the others didn't, or they all may have seen the same things from a different perspective, so when the detectives get all of their stories individually, the details will tend to fit together to give us a more complete picture of what happened. Believe it or not, we will have more total evidence after each witness is interviewed without knowing what the others have said. And the fact that there are apparent differences between the various eyewitness accounts actually is proof that they're telling the truth. If the stories of several witnesses are identical, then we suspect that there was a conspiracy to hide something." Satisfied, the onlooker moved back to the group to share his newly obtained knowledge with the uninitiated.

Within an hour and a half the excitement was over and the deputies, detectives, witnesses, and crowd had all dispersed. Only the cardinal remained undisturbed on her nest. Of course, The Store was closed for the rest of the day and for several days after. Willie decided that it was a good time to take that vacation to the mountains he had been meaning to take but had put off for too long.

The physical evidence was collected and on its way to the sheriff's department to be stored for the district attorney to examine later. The eyewitness accounts would soon be put into a report and all would be prepared for trial pending capture of the man. The details collected from Fred, Judy, Willie, and Jim would prove invaluable, and as a result, unbeknownst to him, Kyle had only another two days before he would begin an enforced detoxification, courtesy of the sheriff's department.

In one short moment Kyle had changed life in the little community of Willow Creek for many months to come. However, thanks to a relative he did not remember but who had been praying for him for several years, the robbery and the events that were to follow would lead Kyle to the point of an even greater change, a change that the young man could never have imagined.

CHAPTER 2
Why Combine the Gospel Accounts?

The four Gospels give us the records of eyewitnesses to the birth, teachings, miracles, death by crucifixion, and bodily resurrection of Jesus of Nazareth. Although Mark and Luke were not eyewitnesses themselves to Jesus' ministry, according to church tradition they recorded the events as told to them by those who were. In the story in chapter one, each of the four eyewitnesses remembered different details and therefore provided different information to the deputies. In the same way, the Gospel writers present varying particulars of specific events because they individually were writing from varying personal perspectives. Also, the Holy Spirit may have simply brought different things to mind especially for the first readers of each Gospel in order to emphasize certain aspects of Jesus as a person and of his ministry.

Even though over the years many people have harmonized the four Gospels, in my opinion it would be very difficult to truly represent a complete timeline of the entire life and ministry of Jesus Christ because the Gospels do not include every detail of each day's events. In John 21:25 the apostle tells us that the recorded events of Jesus' life are only a fraction of all the things He said and did. Usually, only two or three Gospels record a given event and may even record some events in a different order of occurrence, which is not unusual for eyewitness accounts. Other events are to be found in only one Gospel while still others are in all four. Even so, taken together they provide a more complete picture of the teachings and events of Jesus' first coming than any one of them alone would give us.

This is especially true when it is obvious that a single occurrence was recorded in two or more of the gospels. Many of the events in John's Gospel are recorded only there. In the case of Jesus' birth, only Matthew and Luke give us any of the facts. His crucifixion and resurrection are included by all four of the Gospel writers, whereas Jesus' prophecy of His return is recorded only by Matthew, Mark, and Luke. Many of Jesus' teachings are recorded in several of the Gospels but have slight differences. Scholars have noted this fact. Lael Weinberger wrote, "Whatever a first century Jewish teacher like Jesus taught, he would have taught it hundreds of times with minor variations according to his audience. Different gospel writers sometimes recorded different events, which explains many of the alleged contradictions skeptics raise."[1] Interestingly, I didn't know any of these facts until recently. But for no apparent reason, about ten years ago I rediscovered the inconsistencies between the two accounts of Jesus' birth and began to think about their significance. Many years before that, those differences had caused me serious problems.

At Christmas, people usually read the "Christmas Story" from either Matthew or Luke but generally not both because of the differences. On the surface, the two Gospel writers even appear to contradict each other as Weinberger observed. But in II Timothy

---

1   Lael Weinberger, "Assumptions, presumptions and the future of faith," *Journal of Creation* 22 (2008):25.

3:16 the Bible claims to be "inspired by God," meaning that the original documents, written by the authors themselves, included no errors. If there seems to be one, it is only apparent on the surface due to an incomplete understanding of the truth of the accounts.

For example, Matthew mentions only the arrival of the magi while Luke records only the shepherds' visit. This and other facts presented in the two birth narratives have led scholars to make some interesting deductions about the timing of the coming of the magi. But could it be that these deductions are merely assumptions based on the seeming disagreements between the accounts? Through the years most have taught that the magi probably came to Bethlehem to worship Jesus as much as two years after He was born. This assertion is certainly due in part to the magi's apparently having seen a unique star two years before their arrival in Jerusalem (Matthew 2:7) and the resultant murder by Herod of all the children in Bethlehem up to two years of age (Matthew 2:16).

However, Matthew does not tell us when these men began their journey after first having seen the star. Likewise, he does not state their point of origin. They could either have begun a relatively short journey from the area of ancient Babylon or Persia (present day Iraq and Iran, respectively) about one and a half years after the star's appearance (Ezra 7:9 states that the trip from Babylon to Jerusalem took exactly four months), which is the usual assumption made by Bible scholars, or they may have undertaken a much longer journey from the East, perhaps from as far as India or China starting soon after the star was observed. Although the magi most likely came from Babylon or Persia, scholars really do not know.

The term *magi* is used to support Babylon or Persia as their home since that was a term for a pagan priestly group of astronomers/astrologers from that area during the New Testament time period. But the use of that title by Matthew does not require that they came from Babylon or Persia. To put the situation in a current frame of reference, we could imagine that there was a special group of individuals in Canada, known as astronomers, who, as far as anyone in the United States knew, were the only people in the world to examine stars through telescopes. But if one day, to everyone's surprise, a few men of the same occupation came from South America, they would likely also be referred to as astronomers even though they were not from Canada. So the title *magi* does not necessarily specify the nationality of those who came to worship Jesus. A journey from somewhere in central or southern Asia likely would have required most of the two years to prepare for and complete. In either case these men could very well have arrived within at most a few days of Jesus' birth rather than two years later. Although there is no historical or archeological evidence for that possibility, nothing in scripture would prohibit it.

Even though scientists and theologians have speculated about the star of Bethlehem, its true nature is unknown. But it could not have been an ordinary star since, although stars do move through space, their motion would only be observable over a period of centuries if not thousands of years. A star's movement in the sky could not have been detected by human eyes alone over a period of only two years and certainly not in just one night. Matthew 2:9 records that as they left Jerusalem the star "went on before them," moving in the sky as they followed. The most popular explanation, a rare alignment of several planets, would not explain the star for the same reason. The movement of the planets is not detectable in one night. In addition, such an alignment would last only a few days and not two years. Initiating circumstances, both natural and supernatural, and choreographing the activities of individuals in distant parts of the world at different times so that they would come together to be a part of a single event are unmistakable marks of the absolute sovereignty of God over the affairs of mankind.

Matthew states that the magi came "into the house" (Matthew 2:11) to worship Jesus. This reference is also often cited in support of the idea that Jesus was about two years old when the magi arrived, allowing Joseph time to find or build a house for his family, Jesus having been born earlier in the stable of an inn. But a two-year delay in their visit for that reason is not necessary. The Greek word translated "inn" in Luke 2:7 is *kataluma*. In addition to "inn," this word also has the meaning "guest room," which is the way it is translated in Mark 14:14 and Luke 22:11 where it is recorded that Jesus sent his disciples to prepare the "guest room" for the Passover before his crucifixion. This "guest room" is further defined as an "upper room" (Greek *anogeon* meaning "the second floor") in Mark 14:15 and Luke 22:12. The only other time the word "inn" appears in the New Testament is in the parable of the Good Samaritan (Luke 10:34). There it is translated from the Greek *pandocheion* which has only the meaning "inn" or "a place where all are received."

If Joseph was turned away from a commercial inn, why was *pandocheion* not used by Luke? It is possible that there was no room for Joseph and Mary in the upper level guest room of the home of Joseph's relatives or someone else willing to offer lodging, so they were given the use of the stable. In first-century Judea the houses of people who kept farm animals were normally built so that the stable was on the first floor of the house itself with living areas on the upper floor.[2] In that case the magi would have actually come "into the house" to enter the stable, removing the necessity of two years to find permanent housing. Their arrival could have been very soon after Jesus' birth. It was, in fact, this house-versus-stable conflict between Matthew and Luke and the seeming illogic of a two-year delay in the arrival of the magi that first led to the idea of combining the two narratives into one. I did not realize at the time that others had already harmonized the gospels in various forms, although to my knowledge none had combined them into one narrative.

Although scripture does not actually tell us how long it was after Jesus was born that the magi came to worship Him, there are several additional lines of reasoning that indicate that it would probably not have been as long as two years. First, from Matthew 13:55 we know that Joseph was a carpenter in the town of Nazareth. His tools would have been too difficult to carry on a journey of fifty to sixty miles on foot, even if there had been a reason to bring them and especially traveling with a pregnant wife. Granted, he could have returned for the tools, but what reason would cause him to abandon his home as well as his customers in Nazareth to stay in Bethlehem, which probably already had a carpenter? At that time Bethlehem was a small village (Micah 5:2) that would likely not have supported two men of the same trade.

---

[2] "Was Jesus Born in a Stable?" Associates for Biblical Research (1995), <http://christiananswers.net/q-abr/abr-a012.html> (accessed 1997).

Joseph would certainly have planned to go back to Nazareth immediately after his family was enrolled in the census. His livelihood would have demanded their quick return.

Second, if Joseph for some reason had kept Mary and Jesus in Bethlehem for two years, there likely would soon have been a steady stream of the curious to see the new Messiah. Luke 2:17–18 tells us that the wonderful events of that night that were seen and heard by the shepherds were shared with many people they later encountered. In his commentary on Matthew 2:13–15, Matthew Henry says that before the flight to Egypt, Jesus' protection from Herod was "the obscurity he lay in."[3] In other words, Jesus was safe as long as no one knew where He was. It is likely that Herod would have heard of the birth by way of the spreading rumor started by the shepherds and already tried to kill Jesus if he had been born two years prior to the magi's visit. The fact that Herod had not heard until the magi came to Jerusalem would seem to indicate that Jesus' birth had not been long before their arrival, certainly not two years. It would have been important for God's plan of salvation to be completed for His Messiah to disappear from public view soon after His birth until the time was right for His ministry to begin.

But in my opinion the most serious reason against the two-year idea is that it appears to conflict with Luke's information that Joseph and Mary brought Jesus to the temple not long after His birth. Matthew tells us that Joseph heeded the angel's warning about Herod and took Mary and Jesus to Egypt soon after the visit of the magi. Luke states that, according to the requirements in Leviticus 12, Joseph and Mary went to Jerusalem after the

---

[3] http://www.biblestudytools.com/commentaries/matthew-henry-complete/matthew/2.html

time of Mary's purification was completed (forty days following the birth of a son) without mentioning Egypt. For them to have waited two years to do this would have been to disobey the Torah. But because they apparently lived in reverent obedience to God's Law, it seems unlikely that they would have done that. With these and other apparent inconsistencies in the two birth narratives, it is no wonder that both accounts are generally not referenced in great detail in any one sermon. To do so would highlight their seemingly unexplainable conflicts.

On the surface, similar differences exist with the details given in all four of the Gospels concerning the events surrounding the Last Supper and the trial, crucifixion, death, burial, and resurrection of Jesus. There is what seems to be a different order of events or a difference in dialogue spoken, apparently during the same events, between Jesus and His disciples or those who sought His death. Likewise, Jesus' teaching about His return appears to vary among the three who recorded it. Could it be that the Gospel writers had gotten the details of these critical doctrines of Christianity a bit confused? Just as the birth narratives had done, the accounts of the events of the last week of Jesus' life before His crucifixion had caused great confusion and doubt for me in my understanding of the Bible. Which account was true? Or were any of them trustworthy at all?

A letter I received from a Christian ministry included the content of an email from someone who claimed to be an atheist. The skeptic accused the Gospel writers of changing their resurrection narratives. The seeming contradictions between the four Gospels in the details of Jesus' death and resurrection as well as other chronology questions have clearly caused many people to stumble in their faith through the years. Quite possibly one of the most influential people in history to have his faith in scripture damaged by these apparent inaccuracies was none other than Charles Darwin. He wrote the following concerning the cause of his unbelief:

> "[T]he more we know of the fixed laws of nature the more incredible do miracles become,—that the men at that time were ignorant and credulous to a degree almost incomprehensible by us,—that the Gospels cannot be proved to have been written simultaneously with the events,—**that they differ in many important details, far too important as it seemed to me to be admitted as the usual inaccuracies of eyewitnesses;—by such reflections as these ... I gradually came to disbelieve in Christianity as a divine revelation**" (emphasis added).[4]

The man whose very name is given to the notion of evolution apparently had his slide into unbelief accelerated as his doubts about the Gospels grew. Reading the gospels separately at the point of these "important details" would make it difficult to see the differences as anything other than the conflicts he assumed them to be. Of course, it is possible that Darwin's criticism was

---

[4] *The Autobiography of Charles Darwin*, (with original omissions restored, edited with appendix and notes by his granddaughter Nora Barlow) (London: Collins, 1958), 85–96, quoted in "Darwin's arguments against God: How Darwin rejected the doctrines of Christianity" by Russell Grigg, Creation Ministries International, <http://creationontheweb.com/content/view/5703> (accessed September 4, 2008).

leveled at more of the Gospels than just the portions addressed in this book due to what he saw as their unexplainable differences. It also is possible that the supposed conflicts he saw in the Gospels merely gave Darwin an excuse to abandon the Bible and God for the despair of atheism, which helped fuel his naturalistic explanation of the development of life.

But as odd as it may seem, the very skeptics such as Darwin who have pointed to the differences between the Gospels as proof that they are not the inerrant Word of God would likely have been the first to accuse the authors of conspiracy if their accounts had been identical in detail, just as the sheriff's deputies in chapter one would have done to their eyewitnesses if their stories had conformed in every detail. The "differences" between the Gospels actually help confirm their authenticity.

However, none of the above information really explains why I have attempted to combine the separate accounts of these pivotal events in Jesus' first coming as recorded in the Gospels into a single narrative. Ultimately, the reason that I decided to do so is that I wanted to share the fact that not just the Gospels but the entire Bible is completely trustworthy from Genesis to Revelation. This is vitally important to me because I have not always believed it to be true.

My struggles with belief in the truth and authority of scripture actually began in the early 1970s while I was in college studying geology. A psychology student asked me one day why I went to church, and I didn't have a good answer (I have often wondered if I was asked that question as part of a class project designed to "debunk" Christianity). In the back of my mind I had already begun to question my faith and the Bible, particularly the first eleven chapters of Genesis. What I was being taught by my professors about earth's geologic history did not square at all with what the Bible seemed to say. The challenge about church attendance simply brought the doubts into clearer focus.

Having grown up attending church in a nominally Christian family, I wanted to hang on to the Sunday school stories I had heard. As a result, I subconsciously became a theistic evolutionist. That misunderstanding of scripture says that God used evolution to "create" life on the earth over millions of years. Having neatly dispensed with "the Genesis problem," or so I thought, I was faced next with the "obvious conflicts" between the Gospels. The four writers couldn't keep their stories straight, especially John. It appeared that he had been following a different Jesus altogether! From that point my spiritual life began a slow, spiraling descent that continued for years even though I led youth groups, taught Sunday school classes, sang in church choirs, and served as a deacon.

Yet, I didn't come to my crisis point until about fourteen years after graduating from college when I suddenly realized one day that, after having read the Bible regularly for quite a while, I didn't believe it at all. I was stunned by that thought to say the least. How could I not believe the Bible? After all I was a Christian. I went to church. Thankfully, my response was to ask God to show me why. It was a simple and fearful prayer. Not many weeks later, in January 1990, I heard a radio interview with a Ph.D. biologist who was a young-earth creationist. In his discussion he presented simple, scientifically based reasons why evolution was impossible. In an instant of what I can only call revelation I knew that he was correct. Even though I was not blinded by a light from heaven and did not hear an audible voice, the impact of that moment on my life was just as powerful as Saul's encounter with the risen Jesus on his way to Damascus.

My skepticism about the accuracy and truth of scripture had simmered slowly for years after having been taught evolution as unquestioned fact in college. The unbelief that had been born with my complete dismissal of the accounts in Genesis of the Creation, the Fall of Adam and Eve into sin, the global Flood, and the confusion of the languages at the Tower of Babel—and the unbelief that had grown with my doubts about the Gospels—had spread finally to include the entire Bible. But in that instant my unbelief was re-formed into unshakable faith in the full authority of the Bible as the inspired and inerrant Word of God!

Before that encounter with Truth, I had read only sparingly about the creation/evolution controversy. As far as I was concerned, evolution was proven by science. I did not know that evolution has no real scientific basis. In my opinion, creationists were not real scientists. They were uninformed fools (a rather arrogant opinion of credentialed Ph.D. scientists for one who held only a Bachelor of Science degree). The idea that creationists are ignorant non-scientists is still the dominant opinion of creationist scientists among evolutionists.

But as I listened to the interview that day, God showed me that I was the one who had been the fool! I was saved soon after becoming a creationist as I heard the gospel clearly presented for the first time after decades of attending various "evangelical" churches. My indoctrination in evolutionary thinking and running into the seeming conflicts in the Gospels had initiated my unbelief and had been leading me slowly toward atheism.

In the years since the day God changed me from skeptic to believer I have read extensively the scientific literature dealing with origins in almost every field of science written by young-earth creationists as well as some "old-earth creationists" and atheistic evolutionists. Even though I do not have a postgraduate degree myself and am, therefore, not a credentialed scientist, I have come to understand the many scientific arguments for and against the accuracy of the biblical account of earth's early history. The arguments against it are scientifically very weak at best and usually self-contradictory.

I ultimately realized that, since the Bible claims to be the written Word of God, it had to be true that there was a solution to the apparent Gospel conflicts that had helped along the crippling of my faith. Thinking about the importance of law enforcement officers' separately interviewing multiple witnesses of a crime and then combining the accounts, it occurred to me that when the Gospels are read as a single narrative at obvious points of intersection, rather than contradicting each other, Matthew, Mark, Luke, and John might actually provide us with a more complete record of the events surrounding the birth, death, and resurrection of Jesus, including His teaching about His return given on the Mount of Olives. As stated earlier, the idea of "dovetailing" the accounts into one first came to me in relation to the two birth narratives. It was some time later that I attempted to harmonize Jesus' crucifixion and His Olivet Discourse.

Although I also do not have an advanced degree in theology or biblical languages, that fact may actually have made it possible for me to see harmonization as a solution. Sometimes it is possible for a statement made by a respected scholar to become so often repeated that it becomes accepted as fact even though it is merely an opinion. I believe that had I been taught by an authoritative professor of New Testament that Jesus was two years old at the time of the magi's visit it may never have occurred to me that there was a potential explanation for my doubts about the Gospels.

I have combined the Gospel accounts into what seems to be a logical sequence for these events, which are certainly the most important in the first coming of Jesus the Messiah (Christ in Greek). Since the story line jumps between two, three, or four writers, the references of the quoted verses appear in bold type with the references of less informative parallel passages in the other Gospels included in parentheses.

Reading the blended narratives of these events takes them from being disjointed, contradictory stories to a single history that flows, which they in fact are. While I do not claim that the following combinations of the various accounts of these three portions of scripture are in the absolutely correct order in every point, they do, I believe, provide a sequence that harmonizes the Gospels at these three critical places, allowing a single reading of them as they relate the details of these past and future events. The historical and prophetic accuracy of the Gospels, and the Bible as a whole, is after all the truth of the matter.

CHAPTER 3

The Birth of Jesus

Therefore the Lord Himself will give you a sign: Behold, a virgin will be with child and bear a son, and she will call His name Immanuel. Isaiah 7:14

But as for you, Bethlehem Ephrathah, too little to be among the clans of Judah, from you One will go forth for Me to be ruler in Israel. His goings forth are from long ago, from the days of eternity. Micah 5:2

LUKE 1:5–79

In the days of Herod, king of Judea, there was a priest named Zacharias, of the division of Abijah; and he had a wife from the daughters of Aaron, and her name was Elizabeth. 6 They were both righteous in the sight of God, walking blamelessly in all the commandments and requirements of the Lord. 7 But they had no child, because Elizabeth was barren, and they were both advanced in years. 8 Now it happened that while he was performing his priestly service before God in the appointed order of his division, 9 according to the custom of the priestly office, he was chosen by lot to enter the temple of the Lord and burn incense. 10 And the whole multitude of the people were in prayer outside at the hour of the incense offering. 11 And an angel of the Lord appeared to him, standing to the right of the altar of incense. 12 Zacharias was troubled when he saw the angel, and fear gripped him. 13 But the angel said to him, "Do not be afraid, Zacharias, for your petition has been heard, and your wife Elizabeth will bear you a son, and you will give him the name John. 14 You will have joy and gladness, and many will rejoice at his birth. 15 For he will be great in the sight of the Lord; and he will drink no wine or liquor, and he will be filled with the Holy Spirit while yet in his mother's womb. 16 And he will turn many of the sons of Israel back to the Lord their God. 17 It is he who will go as a forerunner before Him in the spirit and power of Elijah, TO TURN THE HEARTS OF THE FATHERS BACK TO THE CHILDREN, and the disobedient to the attitude of the righteous, so as to make ready a people prepared for the Lord." 18 Zacharias said to the angel, "How will I know this for certain? For I am an old man and my wife is advanced in years." 19 The angel answered and said to him, "I am Gabriel, who stands in the presence of God, and I have been sent to speak to you and to bring you this good news. 20 And behold, you shall be silent and unable to speak until the day when these things take place, because you did not believe my words, which will be fulfilled in their proper time." 21 The people were waiting for Zacharias, and were wondering at his delay in the temple. 22 But when he came out, he was unable to speak to them; and they realized that he had seen a vision in the temple; and he kept making signs to them, and remained mute. 23 When the days of his priestly service were ended, he went back home. 24 After these days Elizabeth his wife became pregnant, and she kept herself in seclusion for five months, saying, 25 "This is the way the Lord has dealt with me in the days when He looked with favor upon me, to take away my disgrace among men." 26 Now in the sixth month the angel Gabriel was sent from God to a city in Galilee called Nazareth, 27 to a virgin engaged to a man whose name was Joseph, of the descendants of David; and the virgin's name was Mary. 28 And coming in, he said to her, "Greetings, favored one! The Lord is with you." 29 But she was very perplexed at this statement, and kept pondering what kind of salutation this was. 30 The angel said to her, "Do not be afraid, Mary; for you have found favor with God. 31 And behold, you will conceive in your womb and bear a son, and you shall name Him Jesus. 32 He will be great and will be called the Son of the Most High; and the Lord God will give Him the throne of His father David; 33 and He will reign over the house of Jacob forever, and His kingdom will have no end." 34 Mary said to the angel, "How can this be, since I am a virgin?" 35 The angel answered and said to her, "The Holy

Spirit will come upon you, and the power of the Most High will overshadow you; and for that reason the holy Child shall be called the Son of God. 36 And behold, even your relative Elizabeth has also conceived a son in her old age; and she who was called barren is now in her sixth month. 37 For nothing will be impossible with God." 38 And Mary said, "Behold, the bondslave of the Lord; may it be done to me according to your word." And the angel departed from her. 39 Now at this time Mary arose and went in a hurry to the hill country, to a city of Judah, 40 and entered the house of Zacharias and greeted Elizabeth. 41 When Elizabeth heard Mary's greeting, the baby leaped in her womb; and Elizabeth was filled with the Holy Spirit. 42 And she cried out with a loud voice and said, "Blessed are you among women, and blessed is the fruit of your womb! 43 And how has it happened to me, that the mother of my Lord would come to me? 44 For behold, when the sound of your greeting reached my ears, the baby leaped in my womb for joy. 45 And blessed is she who believed that there would be a fulfillment of what had been spoken to her by the Lord." 46 And Mary said: "My soul exalts the Lord, 47 and my spirit has rejoiced in God my Savior. 48 For He has had regard for the humble state of His bondslave; for behold, from this time on all generations will count me blessed. 49 For the Mighty One has done great things for me; and holy is His name. 50 AND HIS MERCY IS UPON GENERATION AFTER GENERATION TOWARD THOSE WHO FEAR HIM. 51 He has done mighty deeds with His arm; He has scattered those who were proud in the thoughts of their heart. 52 He has brought down rulers from their thrones, and has exalted those who were humble. 53 HE HAS FILLED THE HUNGRY WITH GOOD THINGS; and sent away the rich empty-handed. 54 He has given help to Israel His servant, in remembrance of His mercy, 55 as He spoke to our fathers, to Abraham and his descendants forever." 56 And Mary stayed with her about three months, and then returned to her home. 57 Now the time had come for Elizabeth to give birth, and she gave birth to a son. 58 Her neighbors and her relatives heard that the Lord had displayed His great mercy toward her; and they were rejoicing with her. 59 And it happened that on the eighth day they came to circumcise the child, and they were going to call him Zacharias, after his father. 60 But his mother answered and said, "No indeed; but he shall be called John." 61 And they said to her, "There is no one among your relatives who is called by that name." 62 And they made signs to his father, as to what he wanted him called. 63 And he asked for a tablet and wrote as follows, "His name is John." And they were all astonished. 64 And at once his mouth was opened and his tongue loosed, and he began to speak in praise of God. 65 Fear came on all those living around them; and all these matters were being talked about in all the hill country of Judea. 66 All who heard them kept them in mind, saying, "What then will this child turn out to be?" For the hand of the Lord was certainly with him. 67 And his father Zacharias was filled with the Holy Spirit, and prophesied, saying: 68 "Blessed be the Lord God of Israel, for He has visited us and accomplished redemption for His people, 69 and has raised up a horn of salvation for us in the house of David His servant— 70 as He spoke by the mouth of His holy prophets from of old— 71 salvation FROM OUR ENEMIES, and FROM THE HAND OF ALL WHO HATE US; 72 to show mercy toward our fathers, and to remember His holy covenant, 73 the oath which He swore to Abraham our father, 74 to grant us that we, being rescued from the hand of our enemies, might serve Him without fear, 75 in holiness and righteousness before Him all our days. 76 And you, child, will be called the prophet of the Most High; for you will go on BEFORE THE LORD TO PREPARE HIS WAYS; 77 to give to His people the knowledge of salvation by the forgiveness of their sins, 78 because of the tender mercy of our God, with which the Sunrise from on high will visit us, 79 TO SHINE UPON THOSE WHO SIT IN DARKNESS AND THE SHADOW OF DEATH, to guide our feet into the way of peace."

MATTHEW 1:18–25A

Now the birth of Jesus Christ was as follows: when His mother Mary had been betrothed to Joseph, before they came together she was found to be with child by the Holy

Spirit. 19 And Joseph her husband, being a righteous man and not wanting to disgrace her, planned to send her away secretly. 20 But when he had considered this, behold, an angel of the Lord appeared to him in a dream, saying, "Joseph, son of David, do not be afraid to take Mary as your wife; for the Child who has been conceived in her is of the Holy Spirit. 21 She will bear a Son; and you shall call His name Jesus, for He will save His people from their sins." 22 Now all this took place to fulfill what was spoken by the Lord through the prophet: 23 "BEHOLD, THE VIRGIN SHALL BE WITH CHILD AND SHALL BEAR A SON, AND THEY SHALL CALL HIS NAME IMMANUEL," which translated means, "GOD WITH US." 24 And Joseph awoke from his sleep and did as the angel of the Lord commanded him, and took Mary as his wife, 25a but kept her a virgin until she gave birth to a Son.

LUKE 2:1–21 (MATTHEW 1:25B)

Now in those days a decree went out from Caesar Augustus, that a census be taken of all the inhabited earth. 2 This was the first census taken while Quirinius was governor of Syria. 3 And everyone was on his way to register for the census, each to his own city. 4 Joseph also went up from Galilee, from the city of Nazareth, to Judea, to the city of David which is called Bethlehem, because he was of the house and family of David, 5 in order to register along with Mary, who was engaged to him, and was with child. 6 While they were there, the days were completed for her to give birth. 7 And she gave birth to her firstborn son; and she wrapped Him in cloths, and laid Him in a manger, because there was no room for them in the inn [or, guest room]. 8 In the same region there were some shepherds staying out in the fields and keeping watch over their flock by night. 9 And an angel of the Lord suddenly stood before them, and the glory of the Lord shone around them; and they were terribly frightened. 10 But the angel said to them, "Do not be afraid; for behold, I bring you good news of great joy which will be for all the people; 11 for today in the city of David there has been born for you a Savior, who is Christ the Lord. 12 This will be a sign for you: you will find a baby wrapped in cloths and lying in a manger." 13 And suddenly there appeared with the angel a multitude of the heavenly host praising God and saying, 14 "Glory to God in the highest, and on earth peace among men with whom He is pleased." 15 When the angels had gone away from them into heaven, the shepherds began saying to one another, "Let us go straight to Bethlehem then, and see this thing that has happened which the Lord has made known to us." 16 So they came in a hurry and found their way to Mary and Joseph, and the baby as He lay in the manger. 17 When they had seen this, they made known the statement which had been told them about this Child. 18 And all who heard it wondered at the things which were told them by the shepherds. 19 But Mary treasured all these things, pondering them in her heart. 20 The shepherds went back, glorifying and praising God for all that they had heard and seen, just as had been told them. 21 And when eight days had passed, before His circumcision, His name was then called Jesus, the name given by the angel before He was conceived in the womb.

MATTHEW 2:1–22A

Now after Jesus was born in Bethlehem of Judea in the days of Herod the king, magi from the east arrived in Jerusalem, saying, 2 "Where is He who has been born King of the Jews? For we saw His star in the east and have come to worship Him." 3 When Herod the king heard this, he was troubled, and all Jerusalem with him. 4 Gathering together all the chief priests and scribes of the people, he inquired of them where the Messiah was to be born. 5 They said to him, "In Bethlehem of Judea; for this is what has been written by the prophet: 6 'AND YOU, BETHLEHEM, LAND OF JUDAH, ARE BY NO MEANS LEAST AMONG THE LEADERS OF JUDAH; FOR OUT OF YOU SHALL COME FORTH A RULER WHO WILL SHEPHERD MY PEOPLE ISRAEL.'" 7 Then Herod secretly called the magi and determined from them the exact time the star appeared. 8 And he sent them to Bethlehem and said, "Go and search carefully for the Child; and when you have found Him, report to me, so that I too may come and worship Him." 9 After hearing the king, they went their way; and the star, which they had seen in the east, went on before them until it came and stood over the place where the Child was. 10 When they saw the star, they rejoiced exceedingly with great joy. 11 After coming into the house they saw the Child[5] with Mary His mother; and they fell to the ground and worshiped Him. Then, opening their treasures, they presented to Him gifts of gold, frankincense, and myrrh. 12 And having been warned by God in a dream not to return to Herod, the magi left for their own country by another way. 13 Now when they had gone, behold, an angel of the Lord appeared to Joseph in a dream and said, "Get up! Take the Child and His mother and flee to Egypt, and remain there until I tell you; for Herod is going to search for the Child to destroy Him." 14 So Joseph got up and took the Child and His mother while it was still night, and left for Egypt. 15 He remained there until the death of Herod.[6] This was to fulfill what had been spoken by the Lord through the prophet: "OUT OF EGYPT I CALLED MY SON." 16 Then when Herod saw that he had been tricked by the magi, he became very enraged, and sent and slew all the male children who were in Bethlehem and all its vicinity, from two years old and under, according to the time which he had determined from the magi. 17 Then what had been spoken through Jeremiah the prophet was fulfilled:

---

5   (Matthew 2:11, 13, 14) These references to Jesus as a "young child" (also in verses 8 & 9) are usually taken as further evidence that Jesus was about two years old at this point rather a new-born infant. The Greek word *paidion* used here is a synonym for another Greek word, *brephos*. According to Strong's Exhaustive Concordance, both words have the meaning "infant," "little child," or "young child." Whereas, again according to Strong, *paidion* is not translated as "infant" or "babe" in the New Testament, both *brephos* and *paidion* are used in reference to Jesus as a newborn infant in Luke 2:16–17. Therefore, the use of *paidion* here does not require, or even necessarily imply, that two years had passed before the magi arrived.

6   (Matthew 2:15) According to standard biblical timelines, Herod the Great died in the same year that Jesus was born (about 4 B.C. due to subsequent calendar corrections). There is no reason that his death could not have been within the first 40 days of Jesus' life, allowing Joseph and Mary to carry out the requirements of the Law concerning purification. Maps of Judea at the time of Jesus show that Bethlehem is about 100 miles from the border with Egypt. That distance could have been covered in 8 to 10 days on foot or quicker if both Mary and Joseph rode donkeys. They certainly would have had the financial means in the form of the gifts from the magi with which to purchase any supplies that they would have needed for their escape.

18 "A VOICE WAS HEARD IN RAMAH, WEEPING AND GREAT MOURNING, RACHEL WEEPING FOR HER CHILDREN; AND SHE REFUSED TO BE COMFORTED, BECAUSE THEY WERE NO MORE." 19 But when Herod died, behold, an angel of the Lord appeared in a dream to Joseph in Egypt, and said, 20 "Get up, take the Child and His mother, and go into the land of Israel; for those who sought the Child's life are dead." 21 So Joseph got up, took the Child and His mother, and came into the land of Israel. 22a But when he heard that Archelaus was reigning over Judea in place of his father Herod, he was afraid to go there.

LUKE 2:22–38

And when the days for their purification according to the law of Moses were completed, they brought Him up to Jerusalem to present Him to the Lord 23 (as it is written in the Law of the Lord, "EVERY firstborn MALE THAT OPENS THE WOMB SHALL BE CALLED HOLY TO THE LORD"), 24 and to offer a sacrifice according to what was said in the Law of the Lord, "A PAIR OF TURTLEDOVES OR TWO YOUNG PIGEONS." 25 And there was a man in Jerusalem whose name was Simeon; and this man was righteous and devout, looking for the consolation of Israel; and the Holy Spirit was upon him. 26 And it had been revealed to him by the Holy Spirit that he would not see death before he had seen the Lord's Christ. 27 And he came in the Spirit into the temple; and when the parents brought in the child Jesus, to carry out for Him the custom of the Law, 28 then he took Him into his arms, and blessed God, and said, 29 "Now Lord, You are releasing Your bond-servant to depart in peace, according to Your word; 30 for my eyes have seen Your salvation, 31 which You have prepared in the presence of all peoples, 32 A LIGHT OF REVELATION TO THE GENTILES, and the glory of Your people Israel." 33 And His father and mother were amazed at the things which were being said about Him. 34 And Simeon blessed them and said to Mary His mother, "Behold, this Child is appointed for the fall and rise of many in Israel, and for a sign to be opposed— 35 and a sword will pierce even your own soul—to the end that thoughts from many hearts may be revealed." 36 And there was a prophetess, Anna the daughter of Phanuel, of the tribe of Asher. She was advanced in years and had lived with her husband seven years after her marriage, 37 and then as a widow to the age of eighty-four. She never left the temple, serving night and day with fastings and prayers. 38 At that very moment she came up and began giving thanks to God, and continued to speak of Him to all those who were looking for the redemption of Jerusalem.

MATTHEW 2:22B–23 (LUKE 2:39)

Then after being warned by God in a dream, he [Joseph] left for the regions of Galilee,[7] 23 and came and lived in a city called Nazareth. This was to fulfill what was spoken through the prophets: "He shall be called a Nazarene.

---

7   (Matthew 2:22) While verse 22 seems to say that Joseph did not go to Jerusalem after leaving Egypt, Luke tells us that Joseph and Mary did indeed bring Jesus to the Temple after the time of Mary's purification (40 days as prescribed in Leviticus 12:2–4) to present him to the Lord. As they came into Judea from Egypt, Joseph likely heard that Archelaus was now ruler after his father's death. Apparently Archelaus was known to be more evil and ruthless than his father Herod who had already attempted to kill the Messiah. If so, Joseph would understandably have been afraid to go on to Jerusalem and place Jesus in danger again. The words "turned aside" (Greek *anachoreo*) in the King James Version would seem to imply that Joseph changed course on his way to Jerusalem to instead go to Nazareth in response to his fear. However, the word can also mean "depart." This could imply being in a place to begin with from which to depart. In fact, the King James Version translates *anachoreo* as "departed" in Matthew 2:12 where the magi were "warned of God in a dream that they should not return to Herod, [so] they departed [from Bethlehem where they had just worshiped the infant Jesus] into their own country another way." In addition, the original NASB translates *anachoreo* ("turned aside" in KJV) in Matthew 2:22 as "departed." In light of verse 2:12 and the NASB's translation of 2:22, it may be that Joseph was in a place (Jerusalem, where he had taken Mary and Jesus to the temple) and departed from it to Nazareth, rather than being on the way to that place and turning aside to go to Nazareth. Matthew does not record Joseph's visit to the temple (possibly due to having different sources of information), which could be inserted, as I have done, between 22a and 22b. Though it was not recorded, it may be that God assured Joseph as they traveled toward Jerusalem that they would be safe there so he continued on his way. Later, after visiting the temple as originally planned, being warned in a dream, they departed to Nazareth in "the regions of Galilee."

CHAPTER 4

The Crucifixion, Death, and Resurrection of Jesus

He was oppressed and He was afflicted, yet He did not open His mouth; like a lamb that is led to slaughter, and like a sheep that is silent before its shearers, so He did not open His mouth. Isaiah 53:7

My God, my God, why have You forsaken me? Far from my deliverance are the words of my groaning. Psalm 22:1

For dogs have surrounded me; a band of evildoers has encompassed me; they pierced my hands and my feet. Psalm 22:16

They divide my garments among them, and for my clothing they cast lots. Psalm 22:18

Therefore my heart is glad and my glory rejoices; my flesh also will dwell securely. For You will not abandon my soul to Sheol; nor will You allow Your Holy One to undergo decay. Psalm 16:9–10

JOHN 13:1

Now before the Feast of the Passover, Jesus knowing that His hour had come that He would depart out of this world to the Father, having loved His own who were in the world, He loved them to the end.[8]

---

8   Matthew, Mark, and Luke tell us that Jesus' disciples prepared the Passover on the first day of Unleavened Bread, which was known as the day of preparation for Passover. But all four Gospels say that Jesus was crucified on the day of preparation for the Sabbath. John adds that that Sabbath was also Passover. As a result there is an apparent conflict. Which day was Passover? Tim Hegg, M.Div., Th.M., head of a messianic

LUKE 22:7–16 (MATTHEW 26:17–20, MARK 14:12–17)

Then came the first day of Unleavened Bread on which the Passover lamb had to be sacrificed. 8 And Jesus sent Peter and John, saying, "Go and prepare the Passover for us, so that we may eat it." 9 They said to Him, "Where do You want us to prepare it?" 10 And He said to them, "When you have entered the city, a man will meet you carrying a pitcher of water; follow him into the house that he enters. 11 And you shall say to the owner of the house, 'The Teacher says to you, "Where is the guest room in which I may eat the Passover with My disciples?"' 12 And he will show you a large, furnished upper room; prepare it there." 13 And they left and found everything just as He had told them; and they prepared the Passover.
14 When the hour had come, He reclined at the table, and the apostles with Him. 15 And He said to them, "I have earnestly desired to eat this Passover with you before I suffer; 16 for I say to you, I shall never again eat it until it is fulfilled in the kingdom of God."

JOHN 13:2–25 (MATTHEW 26:21–22, MARK 14:18–19, LUKE 22:23)

During supper, the devil having already put into the heart of Judas Iscariot, the son of Simon, to betray Him, 3 Jesus, knowing that the Father had given all things into His hands, and that He had come forth from God and was going back to God, 4 got up from supper, and laid aside His garments; and taking a towel, He girded Himself. 5 Then He poured water into the basin, and began to wash the disciples' feet and to wipe them with the towel with which He was girded. 6 So He came to Simon Peter. He said to Him, "Lord, do You wash my feet?" 7 Jesus answered

---

Christian ministry called Torah Resource, proposes that Jesus celebrated Passover a day early. The calendar observed by the Essenes was one day ahead of the standard Judean calendar (see http://torahresource.com/EnglishArticles/PassionChronology.pdf for his article). Possibly, since He knew that He was to die on the day before the generally observed Passover, Jesus celebrated the Passover meal with His disciples one day early, also taking the opportunity to institute the Lord's Supper. Perhaps Matthew, Mark, and Luke were citing that variant calendar by simply referring to the day of the preparation of their meal as the first day of Unleavened Bread (the day before Passover) without specifically saying so. Hegg's interpretation does not explain all problems, but it does indicate that there may be other explanations that would do so.

The Crucifixion, Death, and Resurrection of Jesus

and said to him, "What I do you do not realize now, but you will understand hereafter." 8 Peter said to Him, "Never shall You wash my feet!" Jesus answered him, "If I do not wash you, you have no part with Me." 9 Simon Peter said to Him, "Lord, then wash not only my feet, but also my hands and my head." 10 Jesus said to him, "He who has bathed needs only to wash his feet, but is completely clean; and you are clean, but not all of you." 11 For He knew the one who was betraying Him; for this reason He said, "Not all of you are clean." 12 So when He had washed their feet, and taken His garments and reclined at the table again, He said to them, "Do you know what I have done to you? 13 You call Me Teacher and Lord; and you are right, for so I am. 14 If I then, the Lord and the Teacher, washed your feet, you also ought to wash one another's feet. 15 For I gave you an example that you also should do as I did to you. 16 Truly, truly, I say to you, a slave is not greater than his master, nor is one who is sent greater than the one who sent him. 17 If you know these things, you are blessed if you do them. 18 I do not speak of all of you. I know the ones I have chosen; but it is that the Scripture may be fulfilled, 'HE WHO EATS MY BREAD HAS LIFTED UP HIS HEEL AGAINST ME.' 19 From now on I am telling you before it comes to pass, so that when it does occur, you may believe that I am He. 20 Truly, truly, I say to you, he who receives whomever I send receives Me; and he who receives Me receives Him who sent Me." 21 When Jesus had said this, He became troubled in spirit, and testified and said, "Truly, truly, I say to you, that one of you will betray Me." 22 The disciples began looking at one another, at a loss to know of which one He was speaking. 23 There was reclining on Jesus' bosom one of His disciples, whom Jesus loved. 24 So Simon Peter gestured to him, and said to him, "Tell us who it is of whom He is speaking." 25 He, leaning back thus on Jesus' bosom, said to Him, "Lord, who is it?"

MATTHEW 26:23–24 (MARK 14:20–21, LUKE 22:22)

And He answered, "He who dipped his hand with Me in the bowl is the one who will betray Me. 24 The Son of Man is to go, just as it is written of Him; but woe to that man by whom the Son of Man is betrayed! It would have been good for that man if he had not been born."

JOHN 13:26A

Jesus then answered, "That is the one for whom I shall dip the morsel and give it to him."[9]

LUKE 22:21

But behold, the hand of the one betraying Me is with Mine on the table."

MATTHEW 26:25

And Judas, who was betraying Him, said, "Surely it is not I, Rabbi?" Jesus said to him, "You have said it yourself."

JOHN 13:26B–36

So when He had dipped the morsel, He took and gave it to Judas, the son of Simon Iscariot. 27 After the morsel, Satan then entered into him. Therefore Jesus said to him, "What you do, do quickly." 28 Now no one of those reclining at the table knew for what purpose He had said this to him. 29 For some were supposing, because Judas had the money box, that Jesus was saying to him, "Buy the things we have need of for the feast"; or else, that he should give something to the poor. 30 So after receiving the morsel he went out immediately; and it was night. 31 Therefore when he had gone out, Jesus said, "Now is the Son of Man glorified, and God is glorified in Him; 32 if God is glorified in Him, God will also glorify Him in Himself, and will glorify Him immediately. 33 Little children, I am with you a little while longer. You will seek Me; and as I said to the Jews, now I also say to you, 'Where I am going, you

---

9   (John 13:26a) This is not a contradiction with Matthew's and Mark's accounts in that Jesus would likely have timed His giving the morsel (probably a piece of bread) to Judas when Judas had reached into the dish to dip his own morsel. This would have been done so as not to draw attention to what Judas was about to do. If they had known, the disciples might have tried to prevent Judas from carrying out his betrayal of Jesus. As it was, only Peter and John knew the betrayer was Judas.

cannot come.' 34 A new commandment I give to you, that you love one another, even as I have loved you, that you also love one another. 35 By this all men will know that you are My disciples, if you have love for one another." 36 Simon Peter said to Him, "Lord, where are You going?" Jesus answered, "Where I go, you cannot follow Me now; but you will follow later."

LUKE 22:24-32

And there arose also a dispute among them as to which one of them was regarded to be greatest. 25 And He said to them, "The kings of the Gentiles lord it over them; and those who have authority over them are called 'Benefactors.' 26 But it is not this way with you, but the one who is the greatest among you must become like the youngest, and the leader like the servant. 27 For who is greater, the one who reclines at the table or the one who serves? Is it not the one who reclines at the table? But I am among you as the one who serves. 28 You are those who have stood by Me in My trials; 29 and just as My Father has granted Me a kingdom, I grant you 30 that you may eat and drink at My table in My kingdom, and you will sit on thrones judging the twelve tribes of Israel. 31 Simon, Simon, behold, Satan has demanded permission to sift you like wheat; 32 but I have prayed for you, that your faith may not fail; and you, when once you have turned again, strengthen your brothers."

MATTHEW 26:26-29 (MARK 14:22-25, LUKE 22:17-20)

While they were eating, Jesus took some bread, and after a blessing, He broke it and gave it to the disciples, and said, "Take, eat; this is My body." 27 And when He had taken a cup and given thanks, He gave it to them, saying, "Drink from it, all of you; 28 for this is My blood of the covenant, which is poured out for many for forgiveness of sins. 29 But I say to you, I will not drink of this fruit of the vine from now on until that day when I drink it new with you in My Father's kingdom.

JOHN 14:1–18:2 (MATTHEW 26:30, MARK 14:26)

Do not let your heart be troubled; believe in God, believe also in Me. 2 In My Father's house are many dwelling places; if it were not so, I would have told you; for I go to prepare a place for you. 3 If I go and prepare a place for you, I will come again and receive you to Myself, that where I am, there you may be also. 4 And you know the way where I am going." 5 Thomas said to Him, "Lord, we do not know where You are going, how do we know the way?" 6 Jesus said to him, "I am the way, and the truth, and the life; no one comes to the Father but through Me. 7 If you had known Me, you would have known My Father also; from now on you know Him, and have seen Him." 8 Philip said to Him, "Lord, show us the Father, and it is enough for us." 9 Jesus said to him, "Have I been so long with you, and yet you have not come to know Me, Philip? He who has seen Me has seen the Father; how can you say, 'Show us the Father'? 10 Do you not believe that I am in the Father, and the Father is in Me? The words that I say to you I do not speak on My own initiative, but the Father abiding in Me does His works. 11 Believe Me that I am in the Father and the Father is in Me; otherwise believe because of the works themselves. 12 Truly, truly, I say to you, he who believes in Me, the works that I do, he will do also; and greater works than these he will do; because I go to the Father. 13 Whatever you ask in My name, that will I do, so that the Father may be glorified in the Son. 14 If you ask Me anything in My name, I will do it. 15 If you love Me, you will keep My commandments. 16 I will ask the Father, and He will give you another Helper, that He may be with you forever; 17 that is the Spirit of truth, whom the world cannot receive, because it does not see Him or know Him, but you know Him because He abides with you and will be in you. 18 I will not leave you as orphans; I will come to you. 19 After a little while the world will no longer see Me, but you will see Me; because I live, you will live also. 20 In that day you will know that I am in My Father, and you in Me, and I in you. 21 He who has My commandments and keeps them is the one who loves Me; and he who loves Me will be loved by My Father, and I will love him and will disclose Myself to him." 22 Judas (not Iscariot) said to Him, "Lord, what then has happened that You are going to disclose Yourself to us and not to the world?" 23 Jesus answered and said to him, "If anyone loves Me, he will keep My word; and My Father will love him, and We will come to him and make Our abode with him. 24 He who does not love Me does not keep My words; and the word which you hear is not Mine, but the Father's who sent Me. 25 These things I have spoken to you while abiding with you. 26 But the Helper, the Holy Spirit, whom the Father will send in My name, He will teach you all things, and bring to your remembrance all that I said to you. 27 Peace I leave with you; my peace I give to you; not as the world gives do I give to you. Do not let your heart be troubled, nor let it be fearful. 28 You heard that I said to you, 'I go away, and I will come to you.' If you loved Me, you would have rejoiced because I go to the Father, for the Father is greater than I. 29 Now I have told you before it happens, so that when it happens, you may believe. 30 I will not speak much more with you, for the ruler of the world is coming, and he has nothing in Me; 31 but so that the world may know that I love the Father, I do exactly as the Father commanded Me. Get up, let us go from here. 15:1 I am the true vine, and My Father is the vinedresser. 2 Every branch in Me that does not bear fruit, He takes away; and every branch that bears fruit, He prunes it so that it may bear more fruit. 3 You are already clean because of the word which I have spoken to you. 4 Abide in Me, and I in you. As the branch cannot bear fruit of itself unless it abides in the vine, so neither can you unless you abide in Me. 5 I am the vine, you are the branches; he who abides in Me and I in him, he bears much fruit, for apart from Me you can do nothing. 6 If anyone does not abide in Me, he is thrown away as a branch and dries up; and they gather them, and cast them into the fire and they are burned. 7 If you abide in Me, and My words abide in you, ask whatever you wish, and it will be done for you. 8 My Father is glorified by this, that you bear much fruit, and so prove to be My disciples. 9 Just as the Father has loved Me, I have also loved you; abide in My love. 10 If you keep My commandments, you will abide in My love; just as I have kept My Father's commandments and abide in His love. 11 These things I have spoken to you so that My joy may be in you, and that your joy may be made full. 12 This is My commandment, that you love one another, just as I have loved you. 13 Greater love has no one than this, that one lay down his life for his friends. 14 You are My friends if you do what I command you. 15 No longer do I call you slaves, for the slave does not know what his master is doing; but I have called you friends, for all things that I have heard from My Father I have made known to you. 16 You did not choose Me but I chose you, and appointed you that you would go and bear fruit, and that your fruit would remain, so that whatever you ask of the Father in My name He may give to you. 17 This I command you, that you love one another. 18 If the world hates you, you know that it has hated Me before it hated you. 19 If you were of the world, the world would love its own; but because you are not of the world, but I chose you out of the world, because of this the world hates you. 20 Remember the word that I said to you, 'A slave is not greater than his master.' If they persecuted Me, they will also persecute you; if they kept My word, they will keep yours also. 21 But all these things they will do to you for My name's sake, because they do not know the One who sent Me. 22 If I had not come and spoken to them, they would not have sin, but now they have no excuse for their sin. 23 He who hates Me hates My Father also. 24 If I had not done among them the works which no one else did, they would not have sin; but now they have both seen and hated Me and My Father as well. 25 But they have done this to fulfill the word that is written in their Law, 'THEY HATED ME WITHOUT A CAUSE.' 26 When the Helper comes, whom I will send to you from the Father, that is the Spirit of truth who proceeds from the Father, He will testify about Me, 27 and you will testify also, because you have been with Me from the beginning. 16:1 These things I have spoken to you so that you may be kept from stumbling. 2 They will make you outcasts from the synagogue, but an hour is coming for everyone who kills you to think that he is offering service to God. 3 These things they will do because they have not known the Father or Me. 4 But these things I have spoken to you, so that when their hour comes, you may remember that I told you of them. These things I did not say to you at the beginning, because I was with you. 5 But now I am going to Him who sent Me; and none of you asks Me, 'Where are You going?' 6 But because I have said these things to you, sorrow has filled your heart. 7 But I tell you the truth, it is to your advantage that I go away; for if I do not go away, the Helper will not come to you; but if I go, I will send Him to you. 8 And He, when He comes, will convict the world concerning sin and righteousness and judgment; 9 concerning sin, because they do not believe in Me; 10 and concerning righteousness, because I go to the Father and you no longer see Me; 11 and concerning judgment, because the ruler of this world has been judged. 12 I have many more things to say to you, but you cannot bear them now. 13 But when He, the Spirit of truth, comes, He will guide you into all the truth; for He will not speak on His own initiative, but whatever He hears, He will speak; and He will disclose to you what is to come. 14 He will glorify Me, for He will take of Mine and will disclose it to you. 15 All things that the Father has are Mine; therefore I said that He takes of Mine and will disclose it to you. 16 A little while, and you will no longer see Me; and again a little while, and you will see Me." 17 Some of His disciples then said to one another, "What is this thing He is telling us, 'A little while, and you will not see Me; and again a little while, and you will see Me'; and, 'because I go to the Father'?" 18 So they were saying, "What is this that He says, 'A little while'? We do not know what He is talking about." 19 Jesus knew that they wished to question Him, and He said to them, "Are you deliberating together about this, that I said, 'A little while, and you will not see Me, and again a little while, and you will see Me'? 20 Truly, truly, I say to you, that you will weep and lament, but the world will rejoice; you will grieve, but your grief will be turned into joy. 21 Whenever a woman is in labor she has pain, because her hour has come; but when she gives birth to the child, she no longer remembers the anguish because of the joy that a child has been born into the world. 22 Therefore you too have grief now; but I will see you again, and your heart will rejoice, and no one will take your joy away from you. 23 In that day you will not question Me about anything. Truly, truly, I say to you, if you ask the Father for anything in My name, He will give it to you. 24 Until now you have asked for nothing in My name; ask and you will receive, so that your joy may be made full. 25 These things I have spoken to you in figurative language; an hour is coming when I will no longer speak to you in figurative language, but will tell you plainly of the Father. 26 In that day you will ask in My name, and I do not say to you that I will request of the Father on your behalf; 27 for the Father Himself loves you, because you have loved Me and have believed that I came forth from the Father. 28 I came forth from the Father and have come into the world; I am leaving the world again and going to the Father." 29 His disciples said, "Lo, now You are speaking plainly and are not using a figure of speech. 30 Now we know that You know all things, and have no need for anyone to question You; by this we believe that You came from God." 31 Jesus answered them, "Do you now believe? 32 Behold, an hour is coming, and has already come, for you to be scattered, each to his own home, and to leave Me alone; and yet I am not alone, because the Father is with Me. 33 These things I have spoken to you, so that in Me you may have peace. In the world you have tribulation, but take courage; I have overcome the world." 17:1 Jesus spoke these things; and lifting up His eyes to heaven, He said, "Father, the hour has come; glorify Your Son, that the Son may glorify You, 2 even as You gave Him authority over all flesh, that to all whom You have given Him, He may give eternal life. 3 This is eternal life, that they may know You, the only true God, and Jesus Christ whom You have sent. 4 I glorified You on the earth, having accomplished the work which You have given Me to do. 5 Now, Father, glorify Me together with Yourself, with the glory which I had with You before the world was. 6 I have manifested Your name to the men whom You gave Me out of the world; they were Yours and You gave them to Me, and they have kept Your word. 7 Now they have come to know that everything You have given Me is from You; 8 for the words which You gave Me I have given to them; and they received them and truly understood that I came forth from You, and they believed that You sent Me. 9 I ask on their behalf; I do not ask on behalf of the world, but of those whom You have given Me; for they are Yours; 10 and all things that are Mine are Yours, and Yours are Mine; and I have been glorified in them. 11 I am no longer in the world; and yet they themselves are in the world, and I come to You. Holy Father, keep them in Your name, the name which You have given Me, that they may be one even as We are. 12 While I was with them, I was keeping them in Your name which You have given Me; and I guarded them and not one of them perished but the son of perdition, so that the Scripture would be fulfilled. 13 But now I come to You; and these things I speak in the world so that they may have My joy made full in themselves. 14 I have given them Your word; and the world has hated them, because they are not of the world, even as I am not of the world. 15 I do not ask You to take them out of the world, but to keep them from the evil one. 16 They are not of the world, even as I am not of the world. 17 Sanctify them in the truth; Your word is truth. 18 As You sent Me into the world, I also have sent them into the world. 19 For their sakes I sanctify Myself, that they themselves also may be sanctified in truth. 20 I do not ask on behalf of these alone, but for those also who believe in Me through their word; 21 that they may all be one; even as You, Father, are in Me and I in You, that they also may be in Us, so that the world may believe that You sent Me. 22 The glory which You have given Me I have given to them, that they may be one, just as We are one; 23 I in them and You in Me, that they may be perfected in unity, so that the world may know that You sent Me, and loved them, even as You have loved Me. 24 Father, I desire that they also, whom You have given Me, be with Me where I am, so that they may see My glory which You have given Me, for You loved Me before the foundation of the world. 25 O righteous Father, although the world has not known You, yet I have known You; and these have known that You sent Me; 26 and I have made Your name known to them, and will make it known, so that the love with which You loved Me may be in them, and I in them." 18:1 When Jesus had spoken these words, He went forth with His disciples over the ravine of the Kidron, where there was a garden, in which He entered with His disciples. 2 Now Judas also, who was betraying Him, knew the place, for Jesus had often met there with His disciples.

MATTHEW 26:31–32 (MARK 14:27–28)

Then Jesus said to them, "You will all fall away because of Me this night, for it is written, 'I WILL STRIKE DOWN THE SHEPHERD, AND THE SHEEP OF THE FLOCK SHALL BE SCATTERED.' 32 But after I have been raised, I will go ahead of you to Galilee."

MARK 14:29–31 (MATTHEW 26:33–35, LUKE 22:33–34, JOHN 13:37–38)

But Peter said to Him, "Even though all may fall away, yet I will not." 30 And Jesus said to him, "Truly I say to you, that this very night, before a rooster crows twice, you yourself will deny Me three times." 31 But Peter kept saying insistently, "Even if I have to die with You, I will not deny You!" And they all were saying the same thing also.

LUKE 22:35–38

And He said to them, "When I sent you out without money belt and bag and sandals, you did not lack anything, did you?" They said, "No, nothing." 36 And He said to them, "But now, whoever has a money belt is to take it along, likewise also a bag, and whoever has no sword is to sell his coat and buy one. 37 For I tell you that this which is written must be fulfilled in Me, 'AND HE WAS NUMBERED WITH TRANSGRESSORS'; for that which refers to Me has its fulfillment." 38 They said, "Lord, look, here are two swords." And He said to them, "It is enough."

MARK 14:32–36 (MATTHEW 26:36–39, LUKE 22:39–42)

They came to a place named Gethsemane; and He said to His disciples, "Sit here until I have prayed." 33 And He took with Him Peter and James and John, and began to be very distressed and troubled. 34 And He said to them, "My soul is deeply grieved to the point of death; remain here and keep watch." 35 And He went a little beyond them, and fell to the ground and began to pray that if it were possible, the hour might pass Him by. 36 And He was saying, "Abba! Father! All things are possible for You; remove this cup from Me; yet not what I will, but what You will."

LUKE 22:43–44

Now an angel from heaven appeared to Him, strengthening Him. 44 And being in agony He was praying very fervently; and His sweat became like drops of blood, falling down upon the ground.

MARK 14:37–40 (MATTHEW 26:40–43)

And He came and found them sleeping, and said to Peter, "Simon, are you asleep? Could you not keep watch for one hour? 38 Keep watching and praying that you may not come into temptation; the spirit is willing, but the flesh is weak." 39 Again He went away and prayed, saying the same words. 40 And again He came and found them sleeping, for their eyes were very heavy; and they did not know what to answer Him.

MATTHEW 26:44

And He left them again, and went away and prayed a third time, saying the same thing once more.

MARK 14:41–42 (MATTHEW 26:45–46, LUKE 22:45–46)

And He came the third time, and said to them, "Are you still sleeping and resting? It is enough; the hour has come; behold, the Son of Man is being betrayed into the hands of sinners. 42 Get up, let us be going; behold, the one who betrays Me is at hand!"

MATTHEW 26:47–48 (MARK 14:43–44, LUKE 22:47, JOHN 18:3)

While He was still speaking, behold, Judas, one of the twelve, came up accompanied by a large crowd with swords and clubs, who came from the chief priests and elders of the people. 48 Now he who was betraying Him gave them a sign, saying, "Whomever I kiss, He is the one; seize Him."

JOHN 18:4–9

So Jesus, knowing all the things that were coming upon Him, went forth and said to them, "Whom do you seek?" 5 They answered Him, "Jesus the Nazarene." He said to them, "I am He." And Judas also, who was betraying Him, was standing with them. 6 So when He said to them, "I am He," they drew back and fell to the ground. 7 Therefore He again asked them, "Whom do you seek?" And they said, "Jesus the Nazarene." 8 Jesus answered, "I told you that I am He; so if you seek Me, let these go their way," 9 to fulfill the word which He spoke, "Of those whom You have given Me I lost not one."

MATTHEW 26:49–50 (MARK 14:45–46, LUKE 22:48)

Immediately Judas went to Jesus and said, "Hail, Rabbi!" and kissed Him. 50 And Jesus said to him, "Friend, do what you have come for." Then they came and laid hands on Jesus and seized Him.

LUKE 22:49

When those who were around Him saw what was going to happen, they said, "Lord, shall we strike with the sword?"

JOHN 18:10 (MATTHEW 26:51, MARK 14:47, LUKE 22:50)

Simon Peter then, having a sword, drew it and struck the high priest's slave, and cut off his right ear; and the slave's name was Malchus.

LUKE 22:51

But Jesus answered and said, "Stop! No more of this." And He touched his ear and healed him.

MATTHEW 26:52–56 (MARK 14:48–50, LUKE 22:52–53, JOHN 18:11)

Then Jesus said to him, "Put your sword back into its place; for all those who take up the sword shall perish by the sword. 53 Or do you think that I cannot appeal to My Father, and He will at once put at My disposal more than twelve legions of angels? 54 How then will the Scriptures be fulfilled, which say that it must happen this way?" 55 At that time Jesus said to the crowds, "Have you come out with swords and clubs to arrest Me as you would against a robber? Every day I used to sit in the temple teaching and you did not seize Me. 56 But all this has taken place to fulfill the Scriptures of the prophets." Then all the disciples left Him and fled.

MARK 14:51–52

A young man was following Him, wearing nothing but a linen sheet over his naked body; and they seized him. 52 But he pulled free of the linen sheet and escaped naked.

JOHN 18:12–16, 19–24 (MATTHEW 26:57–58, MARK 14:53–54, LUKE 22:54)

So the Roman cohort and the commander and the officers of the Jews, arrested Jesus and bound Him, 13 and led Him to Annas first; for he was father-in-law of Caiaphas, who was high priest that year. 14 Now Caiaphas was the one who had advised the Jews that it was expedient for one man to die on behalf of the people. 15 Simon Peter was following Jesus, and so was another disciple. Now that disciple was known to the high priest, and entered with Jesus into the court of the high priest, 16 but Peter was standing at the door outside. So the other disciple, who was known to the high priest, went out and spoke to the doorkeeper, and brought Peter in. 19 The high priest then questioned Jesus about His disciples, and about His teaching. 20 Jesus answered him, "I have spoken openly to the world; I always taught in synagogues and in the temple, where all the Jews come together; and I spoke nothing in secret. 21 Why do you question Me? Question those who have heard what I spoke to them; they know what I said." 22 When He had said this, one of the officers standing nearby struck Jesus, saying, "Is that the way You answer the high priest?" 23 Jesus answered him, "If I have spoken wrongly, testify of the wrong; but if rightly, why do you strike Me?" 24 So Annas sent Him bound to Caiaphas the high priest.

Luke 22:66

When it was day, the Council of elders of the people assembled, both chief priests and scribes, and they led Him away to their council chamber....

Mark 14:55–60 (Matthew 26:59–62)

Now the chief priests and the whole Council kept trying to obtain testimony against Jesus to put Him to death, and they were not finding any. 56 For many were giving false testimony against Him, but their testimony was not consistent. 57 Some stood up and began to give false testimony against Him, saying, 58 "We heard Him say, 'I will destroy this temple made with hands, and in three days I will build another made without hands.'" 59 Not even in this respect was their testimony consistent. 60 The high priest stood up and came forward and questioned Jesus, saying, "Do You not answer? What is it that these men are testifying against You?"

Matthew 26:63 (Mark 14:61, Luke 22:67a)

But Jesus kept silent. And the high priest said to Him, "I adjure You by the living God, that You tell us whether You are the Christ, the Son of God."

Luke 22:67b–68

But He said to them, "If I tell you, you will not believe; 68 and if I ask a question, you will not answer.

Mark 14:62 (Matthew 26:64, Luke 22:69)

And Jesus said, "I am; and you shall see THE SON OF MAN SITTING AT THE RIGHT HAND OF POWER, and COMING WITH THE CLOUDS OF HEAVEN."

Luke 22:70

And they all said, "Are You the Son of God, then?" And He said to them, "Yes, I am."

MATTHEW 26:65–68 (MARK 14:63–65, LUKE 22:71)

Then the high priest tore his robes and said, "He has blasphemed! What further need do we have of witnesses? Behold, you have now heard the blasphemy; 66 what do you think?" They answered, "He deserves death!" 67 Then they spat in His face and beat Him with their fists; and others slapped Him, 68 and said, "Prophesy to us, You Christ; who is the one who hit You?"

LUKE 22:65

And they were saying many other things against Him, blaspheming.

MARK 14:66–70 (MATTHEW 26:69–73, LUKE 22:55–59, JOHN 18:17–18, 25)

As Peter was below in the courtyard, one of the servant-girls of the high priest came, 67 and seeing Peter warming himself, she looked at him and said, "You also were with Jesus the Nazarene." 68 But he denied it, saying, "I neither know nor understand what you are talking about." And he went out onto the porch. 69 The servant-girl saw him, and began once more to say to the bystanders, "This is one of them!" 70 But again he denied it. And after a little while the bystanders were again saying to Peter, "Surely you are one of them, for you are a Galilean too."

JOHN 18:26

One of the slaves of the high priest, being a relative of the one whose ear Peter cut off, said, "Did I not see you in the garden with Him?"

MARK 14:71–72A (MATTHEW 26:74, LUKE 22:60, JOHN 18:27)

But he began to curse and swear, "I do not know this man you are talking about!" 72a Immediately a rooster crowed a second time.

LUKE 22:61A
The Lord turned and looked at Peter.

MARK 14:72B (MATTHEW 26:75, LUKE 22:61B–62)
And Peter remembered how Jesus had made the remark to him, "Before a rooster crows twice, you will deny Me three times." And he began to weep.

LUKE 22:63–64
Now the men who were holding Jesus in custody were mocking Him and beating Him, 64 and they blindfolded Him and were asking Him, saying, "Prophesy, who is the one who hit You?"

MATTHEW 27:1–11A (MARK 15:1, LUKE 23:1, JOHN 18:28A)
Now when morning came, all the chief priests and the elders of the people conferred together against Jesus to put Him to death; 2 and they bound Him, and led Him away and delivered Him to Pilate the governor. 3 Then when Judas, who had betrayed Him, saw that He had been condemned, he felt remorse and returned the thirty pieces of silver to the chief priests and elders, 4 saying, "I have sinned by betraying innocent blood." But they said, "What is that to us? See to that yourself!" 5 And he threw the pieces of silver into the temple sanctuary and departed; and he went away and hanged himself. 6 The chief priests took the pieces of silver and said, "It is not lawful to put them into the temple treasury, since it is the price of blood." 7 And they conferred together and with the money bought the Potter's Field as a burial place for strangers. 8 For this reason that field has been called the Field of Blood to this day. 9 Then that which was spoken through Jeremiah the prophet was fulfilled: "AND THEY TOOK THE THIRTY PIECES OF SILVER, THE PRICE OF THE ONE WHOSE PRICE HAD BEEN SET by the sons of Israel; 10 AND THEY GAVE THEM FOR THE POTTER'S FIELD, AS THE LORD DIRECTED ME." 11 Now Jesus stood before the governor....

John 18:28b–32

And it was early; and they themselves did not enter into the Praetorium so that they would not be defiled, but might eat the Passover. 29 Therefore Pilate went out to them and said, "What accusation do you bring against this Man?" 30 They answered and said to him, "If this Man were not an evildoer, we would not have delivered Him to you." 31 So Pilate said to them, "Take Him yourselves, and judge Him according to your law." The Jews said to him, "We are not permitted to put anyone to death," 32 to fulfill the word of Jesus which He spoke, signifying by what kind of death He was about to die.

Luke 23:2

And they began to accuse Him, saying, "We found this man misleading our nation and forbidding to pay taxes to Caesar, and saying that He Himself is Christ, a King."

John 18:33–38 (Matthew 27:11b, Mark 15:2, Luke 23:3–4)

Therefore Pilate entered again into the Praetorium, and summoned Jesus and said to Him, "Are You the King of the Jews?" 34 Jesus answered, "Are you saying this on your own initiative, or did others tell you about Me?" 35 Pilate answered, "I am not a Jew, am I? Your own nation and the chief priests delivered You to me; what have You done?" 36 Jesus answered, "My kingdom is not of this world. If My kingdom were of this world, then My servants would be fighting so that I would not be handed over to the Jews; but as it is, My kingdom is not of this realm." 37 Therefore Pilate said to Him, "So You are a king?" Jesus answered, "You say correctly that I am a king. For this I have been born, and for this I have come into the world, to testify to the truth. Everyone who is of the truth hears My voice." 38 Pilate said to Him, "What is truth?" And when he had said this, he went out again to the Jews and said to them, "I find no guilt in Him."

Mark 15:3–5 (Matthew 27:12–14)

The chief priests began to accuse Him harshly. 4 Then Pilate questioned Him again, saying, "Do You not answer?

See how many charges they bring against You!" 5 But Jesus made no further answer; so Pilate was amazed.

LUKE 23:5–16

But they kept on insisting, saying, "He stirs up the people, teaching all over Judea, starting from Galilee even as far as this place." 6 When Pilate heard it, he asked whether the man was a Galilean. 7 And when he learned that He belonged to Herod's jurisdiction, he sent Him to Herod, who himself also was in Jerusalem at that time. 8 Now Herod was very glad when he saw Jesus; for he had wanted to see Him for a long time, because he had been hearing about Him and was hoping to see some sign performed by Him. 9 And he questioned Him at some length; but He answered him nothing. 10 And the chief priests and the scribes were standing there, accusing Him vehemently. 11 And Herod with his soldiers, after treating Him with contempt and mocking Him, dressed Him in a gorgeous robe and sent Him back to Pilate. 12 Now Herod and Pilate became friends with one another that very day; for before they had been enemies with each other. 13 Pilate summoned the chief priests and the rulers and the people, 14 and said to them, "You brought this man to me as one who incites the people to rebellion, and behold, having examined Him before you, I have found no guilt in this man regarding the charges which you make against Him. 15 No, nor has Herod, for he sent Him back to us; and behold, nothing deserving death has been done by Him. 16 Therefore I will punish Him and release Him."

MARK 15:6–10 (MATTHEW 27:15–18, LUKE 23:17–22)

Now at the feast he used to release for them any one prisoner whom they requested. 7 The man named Barabbas had been imprisoned with the insurrectionists who had committed murder in the insurrection. 8 The crowd went up and began asking him to do as he had been accustomed to do for them. 9 Pilate answered them, saying, "Do you want me to release for you the King of the Jews?" 10 For he was aware that the chief priests had handed Him over because of envy.

MATTHEW 27:19-29 (MARK 15:11-18, LUKE 23:23-25, JOHN 18:39-19:3)

While he was sitting on the judgment seat, his wife sent him a message, saying, "Have nothing to do with that righteous Man; for last night I suffered greatly in a dream because of Him." 20 But the chief priests and the elders persuaded the crowds to ask for Barabbas and to put Jesus to death. 21 But the governor said to them, "Which of the two do you want me to release for you?" And they said, "Barabbas." 22 Pilate said to them, "Then what shall I do with Jesus who is called Christ?" They all said, "Crucify Him!" 23 And he said, "Why, what evil has He done?" But they kept shouting all the more, saying, "Crucify Him!" 24 When Pilate saw that he was accomplishing nothing, but rather that a riot was starting, he took water and washed his hands in front of the crowd, saying, "I am innocent of this Man's blood; see to that yourselves." 25 And all the people said, "His blood shall be on us and on our children!" 26 Then he released Barabbas for them; but after having Jesus scourged, he handed Him over to be crucified. 27 Then the soldiers of the governor took Jesus into the Praetorium and gathered the whole Roman cohort around Him. 28 They stripped Him and put a scarlet robe on Him.[10] 29 And after twisting together a crown of thorns, they put it on His head, and a reed in His right hand; and they knelt down before Him and mocked Him, saying, "Hail, King of the Jews!"

MARK 15:19 (MATTHEW 27:30)

They kept beating His head with a reed, and spitting on Him, and kneeling and bowing before Him.

JOHN 19:4-15

Pilate came out again and said to them, "Behold, I am bringing Him out to you so that you may know that I find no guilt in Him." 5 Jesus then came out, wearing the crown of thorns and the purple robe.[11] Pilate said to them,

---

10 (Matthew 27:28) Possibly the robe put on Jesus by Herod's soldiers.
11 (John 19:5 and Mark 15:20) While Matthew 27:28 describes the robe as scarlet, the Greek word translated as purple in Mark's and John's passages (*porphura*)

"Behold, the Man!" 6 So when the chief priests and the officers saw Him, they cried out saying, "Crucify, crucify!" Pilate said to them, "Take Him yourselves and crucify Him, for I find no guilt in Him." 7 The Jews answered him, "We have a law, and by that law He ought to die because He made Himself out to be the Son of God." 8 Therefore when Pilate heard this statement, he was even more afraid; 9 and he entered into the Praetorium again and said to Jesus, "Where are You from?" But Jesus gave him no answer. 10 So Pilate said to Him, "You do not speak to me? Do You not know that I have authority to release You, and I have authority to crucify You?" 11 Jesus answered, "You would have no authority over Me, unless it had been given you from above; for this reason he who delivered Me to you has the greater sin." 12 As a result of this Pilate made efforts to release Him, but the Jews cried out saying, "If you release this Man, you are no friend of Caesar; everyone who makes himself out to be a king opposes Caesar." 13 Therefore when Pilate heard these words, he brought Jesus out, and sat down on the judgment seat at a place called The Pavement, but in Hebrew, Gabbatha. 14 Now it was the day of preparation for the Passover; it was about the sixth hour.[12] And he said to the Jews, "Behold, your King!" 15 So they cried out, "Away with Him, away with Him, crucify Him!" Pilate said to them, "Shall I crucify your King?" The chief priests answered, "We have no king but Caesar."

---

is the name of a mussel that produces a reddish-purple dye (*The Complete Word Study Dictionary New Testament*, Spiros Zodhiates, Th.D., ed., AMG Publishers, Chattanooga, TN, 1203). The different color names could simply have resulted from the subjectivity of the observers perhaps seeing the robe in different light.

12   (John 19:14) John records here that it was the "sixth hour" when Pilate passed judgment on Jesus for him to be crucified. Mark 15:25 states that it was the "third hour" when Jesus was actually crucified. Matthew 27:45 and Luke 23:44 say that it became dark from the "sixth hour" to the "ninth hour." The conflict with the time of events disappears with the fact that the Romans began numbering the hours at midnight as we do, whereas the Jews began numbering the daylight hours at sunrise. So Pilate condemned Jesus to death at about 6:00 a.m., Jesus was crucified at about 9:00 a.m. and darkness fell on the land from about noon until 3:00 p.m.

MARK 15:20 (MATHEW 27:31)

After they had mocked Him, they took the purple robe off Him and put His own garments on Him. And they led Him out to crucify Him.

LUKE 23:26–32 (MATTHEW 27:32, MARK 15:21, JOHN 19:16)

When they led Him away, they seized a man, Simon of Cyrene, coming in from the country, and placed on him the cross to carry behind Jesus. 27 And following Him was a large crowd of the people, and of women who were mourning and lamenting Him. 28 But Jesus turning to them said, "Daughters of Jerusalem, stop weeping for Me, but weep for yourselves and for your children. 29 For behold, the days are coming when they will say, 'Blessed are the barren, and the wombs that never bore, and the breasts that never nursed.' 30 Then they will begin TO SAY TO THE MOUNTAINS, 'FALL ON US,' AND TO THE HILLS, 'COVER US.' 31 For if they do these things when the tree is green, what will happen when it is dry?" 32 Two others also, who were criminals, were being led away to be put to death with Him.

MARK 15:22–23, 25 (MATTHEW 27:33–34, LUKE 23:33A, JOHN 19:17)

Then they brought Him to the place Golgotha, which is translated, Place of a Skull. 23 They tried to give Him wine mixed with myrrh; but He did not take it.
25 And it was the third hour when they crucified Him.

JOHN 19:19–22 (MATTHEW 27:35–37, MARK 15:26, LUKE 23:38)

Pilate also wrote an inscription and put it on the cross. It was written, "JESUS THE NAZARENE, THE KING OF THE JEWS." 20 Therefore many of the Jews read this inscription, for the place where Jesus was crucified was near the city; and it was written in Hebrew, Latin and in Greek. 21 So the chief priests of the Jews were saying to Pilate, "Do not write, 'The King of the Jews'; but that He said, 'I am King of the Jews.'" 22 Pilate answered, "What I have written I have written."

Luke 23:34a

But Jesus was saying, "Father, forgive them; for they do not know what they are doing."

John 19:23–27 (Mark 15:24, Luke 23:34b)

Then the soldiers, when they had crucified Jesus, took His outer garments and made four parts, a part to every soldier and also the tunic; now the tunic was seamless, woven in one piece. 24 So they said to one another, "Let us not tear it, but cast lots for it, to decide whose it shall be"; this was to fulfill the Scripture: "THEY DIVIDED MY OUTER GARMENTS AMONG THEM, AND FOR MY CLOTHING THEY CAST LOTS." 25 Therefore the soldiers did these things. But standing by the cross of Jesus were His mother, and His mother's sister, Mary the wife of Clopas, and Mary Magdalene. 26 When Jesus then saw His mother, and the disciple whom He loved standing nearby, He said to His mother, "Woman, behold, your son!" 27 Then He said to the disciple, "Behold, your mother!" From that hour the disciple took her into his own household.

Mark 15:27–28 (Matthew 27:38, Luke 23:33b, John 19:18)

They crucified two robbers with Him, one on His right and one on His left. 28 And the Scripture was fulfilled which says, "And He was numbered with transgressors."

Matthew 27:39–44 (Mark 15:29–32, Luke 23:35)

And those passing by were hurling abuse at Him, wagging their heads 40 and saying, "You who are going to destroy the temple and rebuild it in three days, save Yourself! If You are the Son of God, come down from the cross." 41 In the same way the chief priests also, along with the scribes and elders, were mocking Him and saying, 42 "He saved others; He cannot save Himself. He is the King of Israel; let Him now come down from the cross, and we will believe in Him. 43 HE TRUSTS IN GOD; LET GOD RESCUE Him now, IF HE DELIGHTS IN HIM; for He said, 'I am the Son of God.'"

44 The robbers who had been crucified with Him were also insulting Him with the same words.

LUKE 23:36-37, 39-43

The soldiers also mocked Him, coming up to Him, offering Him sour wine, 37 and saying, "If You are the King of the Jews, save Yourself!" 39 One of the criminals who were hanged there was hurling abuse at Him, saying, "Are You not the Christ? Save Yourself and us!" 40 But the other answered, and rebuking him said, "Do you not even fear God, since you are under the same sentence of condemnation? 41 And we indeed are suffering justly, for we are receiving what we deserve for our deeds; but this man has done nothing wrong." 42 And he was saying, "Jesus, remember me when You come in Your kingdom!" 43 And He said to him, "Truly I say to you, today you shall be with Me in Paradise."

MATTHEW 27:45-47 (MARK 15:33-35, LUKE 23:44-45A)

Now from the sixth hour darkness fell upon all the land until the ninth hour. 46 About the ninth hour Jesus cried out with a loud voice, saying, "ELI, ELI, LAMA SABACHTHANI?" that is, "MY GOD, MY GOD, WHY HAVE YOU FORSAKEN ME?" 47 And some of those who were standing there, when they heard it, began saying, "This man is calling for Elijah."

JOHN 19:28

After this, Jesus, knowing that all things had already been accomplished, to fulfill the Scripture, said, "I am thirsty."

MATTHEW 27:48-49 (MARK 15:36, JOHN 19:29)

Immediately one of them ran, and taking a sponge, he filled it with sour wine and put it on a reed, and gave Him a drink. 49 But the rest of them said, "Let us see whether Elijah will come to save Him."

Luke 23:46a

And Jesus, crying out with a loud voice, said, "Father, INTO YOUR HANDS I COMMIT MY SPIRIT."

John 19:30 (Matthew 27:50, Mark 15:37, Luke 23:46b)

Therefore when Jesus had received the sour wine, He said, "It is finished!" And He bowed His head and gave up His spirit.

Matthew 27:51–56 (Mark 15:38–41, Luke 23:45b, 47–49)

And behold, the veil of the temple was torn in two from top to bottom; and the earth shook and the rocks were split. 52 The tombs were opened, and many bodies of the saints who had fallen asleep were raised; 53 and coming out of the tombs after His resurrection they entered the holy city and appeared to many. 54 Now the centurion, and those who were with him keeping guard over Jesus, when they saw the earthquake and the things that were happening, became very frightened and said, "Truly this was the Son of God!" 55 Many women were there looking on from a distance, who had followed Jesus from Galilee while ministering to Him. 56 Among them was Mary Magdalene, and Mary the mother of James and Joseph, and the mother of the sons of Zebedee.

John 19:31–37

Then the Jews, because it was the day of preparation, so that the bodies would not remain on the cross on the Sabbath (for that Sabbath was a high day), asked Pilate that their legs might be broken, and that they might be taken away. 32 So the soldiers came, and broke the legs of the first man and of the other who was crucified with Him; 33 but coming to Jesus, when they saw that He was already dead, they did not break His legs. 34 But one of the soldiers pierced His side with a spear, and immediately blood and water came out. 35 And he who has seen has testified, and his testimony is true; and he knows that he is telling the truth, so that you also may believe. 36 For these things came to pass to fulfill the Scripture,

"NOT A BONE OF HIM SHALL BE BROKEN." 37 And again another Scripture says, "THEY SHALL LOOK ON HIM WHOM THEY PIERCED."

MARK 15:42–45 (MATTHEW 27:57–58, LUKE 23:50–52, 54, JOHN 19:38)

When evening had already come, because it was the preparation day, that is, the day before the Sabbath, 43 Joseph of Arimathea came, a prominent member of the Council, who himself was waiting for the kingdom of God; and he gathered up courage and went in before Pilate, and asked for the body of Jesus. 44 Pilate wondered if He was dead by this time, and summoning the centurion, he questioned him as to whether He was already dead. 45 And ascertaining this from the centurion, he granted the body to Joseph.

JOHN 19:39–42 (MATTHEW 27:59–60, MARK 15:46, LUKE 23:53)

Nicodemus, who had first come to Him by night, also came, bringing a mixture of myrrh and aloes, about a hundred pounds weight. 40 So they took the body of Jesus and bound it in linen wrappings with the spices, as is the burial custom of the Jews. 41 Now in the place where He was crucified there was a garden, and in the garden a new tomb in which no one had yet been laid. 42 Therefore because of the Jewish day of preparation, since the tomb was nearby, they laid Jesus there.

MARK 15:47 (MATTHEW 27:61, LUKE 23:55)

Mary Magdalene and Mary the mother of Joses were looking on to see where He was laid.

LUKE 23:56

Then they returned and prepared spices and perfumes. And on the Sabbath they rested according to the commandment.

Matthew 27:62–66

Now on the next day, the day after the preparation, the chief priests and the Pharisees gathered together with Pilate, 63 and said, "Sir, we remember that when He was still alive that deceiver said, 'After three days I am to rise again.' 64 Therefore, give orders for the grave to be made secure until the third day, otherwise His disciples may come and steal Him away and say to the people, 'He has risen from the dead,' and the last deception will be worse than the first." 65 Pilate said to them, "You have a guard; go, make it as secure as you know how." 66 And they went and made the grave secure, and along with the guard they set a seal on the stone.

Mark 16:1

When the Sabbath was over, Mary Magdalene, and Mary the mother of James, and Salome, bought spices that they might come and anoint Him.[13]

John 20:1–18 (Matthew 28:1, Luke 24:12)

Now on the first day of the week Mary Magdalene came early to the tomb, while it was still dark, and saw the stone already taken away from the tomb.[14] 2 So she ran and

---

13   Possibly, seeing that they didn't have enough spices, after the Sabbath ended at sunset they bought more.

14   (John 20:1) John records that Mary Magdalene came to the tomb before dawn. Without going inside she ran to tell Peter and John that Jesus' body had been moved. Matthew 28:1 adds that the other Mary came with her, which would explain Mary's comment in John 20:2 that "we do not know where they have laid Him." Peter and John came to the tomb then left before anyone else arrived and before Jesus showed himself to Mary Magdalene who had followed them. Mark includes Mary Magdalene in a list of women who bought spices but doesn't say that she was with them when they came to the tomb. Mark 16:2 says that the women didn't arrive until after sunrise. Mary Magdalene and the mother of James could not have been with them since they discussed the stone and the two Marys would have known that it was moved. Luke includes Mary Magdalene in his list of the women who came with the spices, perhaps because in the reports he later received about Jesus' resurrection all of the women who came to the tomb were listed together. Again, all of the accounts combined give a more complete order of events.

came to Simon Peter and to the other disciple whom Jesus loved, and said to them, "They have taken away the Lord out of the tomb, and we do not know where they have laid Him." 3 So Peter and the other disciple went forth, and they were going to the tomb. 4 The two were running together; and the other disciple ran ahead faster than Peter and came to the tomb first; 5 and stooping and looking in, he saw the linen wrappings lying there; but he did not go in. 6 And so Simon Peter also came, following him, and entered the tomb; and he saw the linen wrappings lying there, 7 and the face-cloth which had been on His head, not lying with the linen wrappings, but rolled up in a place by itself. 8 So the other disciple who had first come to the tomb then also entered, and he saw and believed. 9 For as yet they did not understand the Scripture, that He must rise again from the dead. 10 So the disciples went away again to their own homes. 11 But Mary was standing outside the tomb weeping; and so, as she wept, she stooped and looked into the tomb; 12 and she saw two angels in white sitting, one at the head and one at the feet, where the body of Jesus had been lying. 13 And they said to her, "Woman, why are you weeping?" She said to them, "Because they have taken away my Lord, and I do not know where they have laid Him." 14 When she had said this, she turned around and saw Jesus standing there, and did not know that it was Jesus. 15 Jesus said to her, "Woman, why are you weeping? Whom are you seeking?" Supposing Him to be the gardener, she said to Him, "Sir, if you have carried Him away, tell me where you have laid Him, and I will take Him away." 16 Jesus said to her, "Mary!" She turned and said to Him in Hebrew, "Rabboni!" (which means, Teacher). 17 Jesus said to her, "Stop clinging to Me, for I have not yet ascended to the Father; but go to My brethren and say to them, 'I ascend to My Father and your Father, and My God and your God.'" 18 Mary Magdalene came, announcing to the disciples, "I have seen the Lord," and that He had said these things to her.

LUKE 24:1 (MARK 16:2)

But on the first day of the week, at early dawn, they came to the tomb bringing the spices which they had prepared.[15]

MATTHEW 28:2–4

And behold, a severe earthquake had occurred, for an angel of the Lord descended from heaven and came and rolled away the stone and sat upon it. 3 And his appearance was like lightning, and his clothing as white as snow. 4 The guards shook for fear of him and became like dead men.

MARK 16:3–4 (LUKE 24:2–3)

They [the women] were saying to one another, "Who will roll away the stone for us from the entrance of the tomb?" 4 Looking up, they saw that the stone had been rolled away, although it was extremely large.

LUKE 24:4 (MARK 16:5)

While they were perplexed about this, behold, two men suddenly stood near them in dazzling clothing;

MATTHEW 28:5

The angel said to the women, "Do not be afraid; for I know that you are looking for Jesus who has been crucified."

LUKE 24:5–8 (MATTHEW 28:6)

And as the women were terrified and bowed their faces to the ground, the men said to them, "Why do you seek the living One among the dead? 6 He is not here, but He has risen. Remember how He spoke to you while He was still in Galilee, 7 saying that the Son of Man must be delivered into the hands of sinful men, and be crucified, and the third day rise again." 8 And they remembered His words.

---

15   (Luke 24:1) "They" in this passage would not have included Mary Magdalene and the other Mary who had gone to the tomb without the others before sunrise on Sunday.

MARK 16:6-7 (MATTHEW 28:7)

And he said to them, "Do not be amazed; you are looking for Jesus the Nazarene, who has been crucified. He has risen; He is not here; behold, here is the place where they laid Him. 7 But go, tell His disciples and Peter, 'He is going ahead of you to Galilee; there you will see Him, just as He told you.'"

MATTHEW 28:8-15 (MARK 16:8, LUKE 24:9)

And they left the tomb quickly with fear and great joy and ran to report it to His disciples. 9 And behold, Jesus met them and greeted them. And they came up and took hold of His feet and worshiped Him. 10 Then Jesus said to them, "Do not be afraid; go and take word to My brethren to leave for Galilee, and there they will see Me." 11 Now while they were on their way, some of the guard came into the city and reported to the chief priests all that had happened. 12 And when they had assembled with the elders and consulted together, they gave a large sum of money to the soldiers, 13 and said, "You are to say, 'His disciples came by night and stole Him away while we were asleep.' 14 And if this should come to the governor's ears, we will win him over and keep you out of trouble." 15 And they took the money and did as they had been instructed; and this story was widely spread among the Jews, and is to this day.

LUKE 24:10-11, 13-43 (MARK 16:9-14, JOHN 20:19-20)

Now they were Mary Magdalene and Joanna and Mary the mother of James; also the other women with them were telling these things to the apostles. 11 But these words appeared to them as nonsense, and they would not believe them. 13 And behold, two of them were going that very day to a village named Emmaus, which was about seven miles from Jerusalem. 14 And they were talking with each other about all these things which had taken place. 15 While they were talking and discussing, Jesus Himself approached and began traveling with them. 16 But their eyes were prevented from recognizing Him. 17 And He said to them, "What are these words that you are exchanging with one another as you are walking?" And they stood still, looking sad. 18 One of them, named Cleopas, answered and said to Him, "Are You the only one visiting Jerusalem and unaware of the things which have happened here in these days?" 19 And He said to them, "What things?" And they said to Him, "The things about Jesus the Nazarene, who was a prophet mighty in deed and word in the sight of God and all the people, 20 and how the chief priests and our rulers delivered Him to the sentence of death, and crucified Him. 21 But we were hoping that it was He who was going to redeem Israel. Indeed, besides all this, it is the third day since these things happened. 22 But also some women among us amazed us. When they were at the tomb early in the morning, 23 and did not find His body, they came, saying that they had also seen a vision of angels who said that He was alive. 24 Some of those who were with us went to the tomb and found it just exactly as the women also had said; but Him they did not see." 25 And He said to them, "O foolish men and slow of heart to believe in all that the prophets have spoken! 26 Was it not necessary for the Christ to suffer these things and to enter into His glory?" 27 Then beginning with Moses and with all the prophets, He explained to them the things concerning Himself in all the Scriptures. 28 And they approached the village where they were going, and He acted as though He were going farther. 29 But they urged Him, saying, "Stay with us, for it is getting toward evening, and the day is now nearly over." So He went in to stay with them. 30 When He had reclined at the table with them, He took the bread and blessed it, and breaking it, He began giving it to them. 31 Then their eyes were opened and they recognized Him; and He vanished from their sight. 32 They said to one another, "Were not our hearts burning within us while He was speaking to us on the road, while He was explaining the Scriptures to us?" 33 And they got up that very hour and returned to Jerusalem, and found gathered together the eleven and those who were with them, 34 saying, "The Lord has really risen and has appeared to Simon." 35 They began to relate their experiences on the road and how He was recognized by them in the breaking of the bread. 36 While they were telling these things, He Himself stood in their midst and said to them, "Peace be to you." 37 But they were startled and frightened and thought that they were seeing a spirit. 38 And He said to them, "Why are you troubled, and why do doubts arise in your hearts? 39 See My hands and My feet, that it is I Myself; touch Me and see, for a spirit does not have flesh and bones as you see that I have." 40 And when He had said this, He showed them His hands and His feet. 41 While they still could not believe it because of their joy and amazement, He said to them, "Have you anything here to eat?" 42 They gave Him a piece of a broiled fish; 43 and He took it and ate it before them.

JOHN 20:21–29

So Jesus said to them again, "Peace be with you; as the Father has sent Me, I also send you." 22 And when He had said this, He breathed on them and said to them, "Receive the Holy Spirit. 23 If you forgive the sins of any, their sins have been forgiven them; if you retain the sins of any, they have been retained." 24 But Thomas, one of the twelve, called Didymus, was not with them when Jesus came. 25 So the other disciples were saying to him, "We have seen the Lord!" But he said to them, "Unless I see in His hands the imprint of the nails, and put my finger into the place of the nails, and put my hand into His side, I will not believe." 26 After eight days His disciples were again inside, and Thomas with them. Jesus came, the doors having been shut, and stood in their midst and said, "Peace be with you." 27 Then He said to Thomas, "Reach here with your finger, and see My hands; and reach here your hand and put it into My side; and do not be unbelieving, but believing." 28 Thomas answered and said to Him, "My Lord and my God!" 29 Jesus said to him, "Because you have seen Me, have you believed? Blessed are they who did not see, and yet believed."

MATTHEW 28:16–20 (MARK 16:15–18)

But the eleven disciples proceeded to Galilee, to the mountain which Jesus had designated. 17 When they saw Him, they worshiped Him; but some were doubtful. 18 And Jesus came up and spoke to them, saying, "All authority has been given to Me in heaven and on earth. 19 Go therefore and make disciples of all the nations, baptizing them in the name of the Father and the Son and the Holy Spirit, 20 teaching them to observe all that I commanded you; and lo, I am with you always, even to the end of the age."

John 21:1-24

After these things Jesus manifested Himself again to the disciples at the Sea of Tiberias, and He manifested Himself in this way. 2 Simon Peter, and Thomas called Didymus, and Nathanael of Cana in Galilee, and the sons of Zebedee, and two others of His disciples were together. 3 Simon Peter said to them, "I am going fishing." They said to him, "We will also come with you." They went out and got into the boat; and that night they caught nothing. 4 But when the day was now breaking, Jesus stood on the beach; yet the disciples did not know that it was Jesus. 5 So Jesus said to them, "Children, you do not have any fish, do you?" They answered Him, "No." 6 And He said to them, "Cast the net on the right-hand side of the boat and you will find a catch." So they cast, and then they were not able to haul it in because of the great number of fish. 7 Therefore that disciple whom Jesus loved said to Peter, "It is the Lord." So when Simon Peter heard that it was the Lord, he put his outer garment on (for he was stripped for work), and threw himself into the sea. 8 But the other disciples came in the little boat, for they were not far from the land, but about one hundred yards away, dragging the net full of fish. 9 So when they got out on the land, they saw a charcoal fire already laid and fish placed on it, and bread. 10 Jesus said to them, "Bring some of the fish which you have now caught." 11 Simon Peter went up and drew the net to land, full of large fish, a hundred and fifty-three; and although there were so many, the net was not torn. 12 Jesus said to them, "Come and have breakfast." None of the disciples ventured to question Him, "Who are You?" knowing that it was the Lord. 13 Jesus came and took the bread and gave it to them, and the fish likewise. 14 This is now the third time that Jesus was manifested to the disciples, after He was raised from the dead. 15 So when they had finished breakfast, Jesus said to Simon Peter, "Simon, son of John, do you love Me more than these?" He said to Him, "Yes, Lord; You know that I love You." He said to him, "Tend My lambs." 16 He said to him again a second time, "Simon, son of John, do you love Me?" He said to Him, "Yes, Lord; You know that I love You." He said to him, "Shepherd My sheep." 17 He said to him the third time, "Simon, son of John, do you love Me?" Peter was grieved because He said to him the third time, "Do you love Me?" And he said to Him, "Lord, You know all things; You know that I love You." Jesus said to him, "Tend My sheep. 18 Truly, truly, I say to you, when you were younger, you used to gird yourself and walk wherever you wished; but when you grow old, you will stretch out your hands and someone else will gird you, and bring you where you do not wish to go." 19 Now this He said, signifying by what kind of death he would glorify God. And when He had spoken this, He said to him, "Follow Me!" 20 Peter, turning around, saw the disciple whom Jesus loved following them; the one who also had leaned back on His bosom at the supper and said, "Lord, who is the one who betrays You?" 21 So Peter seeing him said to Jesus, "Lord, and what about this man?" 22 Jesus said to him, "If I want him to remain until I come, what is that to you? You follow Me!" 23 Therefore this saying went out among the brethren that that disciple would not die; yet Jesus did not say to him that he would not die, but only, "If I want him to remain until I come, what is that to you?" 24 This is the disciple who is testifying to these things and wrote these things, and we know that his testimony is true.

LUKE 24:44-53 (MARK 16:19)

Now He said to them, "These are My words which I spoke to you while I was still with you, that all things which are written about Me in the Law of Moses and the Prophets and the Psalms must be fulfilled." 45 Then He opened their minds to understand the Scriptures, 46 and He said to them, "Thus it is written, that the Christ would suffer and rise again from the dead the third day, 47 and that repentance for forgiveness of sins would be proclaimed in His name to all the nations, beginning from Jerusalem. 48 You are witnesses of these things. 49 And behold, I am sending forth the promise of My Father upon you; but you are to stay in the city until you are clothed with power from on high." 50 And He led them out as far as Bethany, and He lifted up His hands and blessed them. 51 While He was blessing them, He parted from them and was carried up into heaven. 52 And they, after worshiping Him, returned to Jerusalem with great joy, 53 and were continually in the temple praising God.

MARK 16:20A

And they went out and preached everywhere, while the Lord worked with them, and confirmed the word by the signs that followed.

JOHN 20:30–31, 21:25

Therefore many other signs Jesus also performed in the presence of the disciples, which are not written in this book; 31 but these have been written so that you may believe that Jesus is the Christ, the Son of God; and that believing you may have life in His name. 21:25 And there are also many other things which Jesus did, which if they were written in detail, I suppose that even the world itself would not contain the books

CHAPTER 5

The Second Coming of Jesus

> *I kept looking in the night visions, and behold, with the clouds of heaven One like a Son of Man was coming, and He came up to the Ancient of Days and was presented before Him.* Daniel 7:13

> *And then the sign of the Son of Man will appear in the sky, and then all the tribes of the earth will mourn, and they will see the SON OF MAN COMING ON THE CLOUDS OF THE SKY with power and great glory.* Matthew 24:30

Although the following events including Jesus' teachings concerning His Second Coming actually occurred several days before His crucifixion, it seemed appropriate to place them after that narrative, since His return will bring this age to an end. The accounts recorded by Matthew and Mark are similar, but Luke includes Jesus' prediction of the destruction of Jerusalem and the temple accomplished by the Roman army led by Titus in 70 A.D.

MARK 13:1-3 (MATTHEW 24:1-3A, LUKE 21:5-6)

As He was going out of the temple, one of His disciples said to Him, "Teacher, behold what wonderful stones and what wonderful buildings!" 2 And Jesus said to him, "Do you see these great buildings? Not one stone will be left upon another which will not be torn down." 3 As He was sitting on the Mount of Olives opposite the temple, Peter and James and John and Andrew were questioning Him privately,

MATTHEW 24:3B–6 (MARK 13:4–7, LUKE 21:7–9)

"Tell us, when will these happen, and what will be the sign of Your coming, and of the end of the age?" 4 And Jesus answered and said to them, "See to it that no one misleads you. 5 For many will come in My name, saying, 'I am the Christ,' and will mislead many. 6 You will be hearing of wars and rumors of wars. See that you are not frightened, for those things must take place, but that is not yet the end."

LUKE 21:10–11 (MATTHEW 24:7, MARK 13:8A)

Then He continued by saying to them, "Nation will rise against nation and kingdom against kingdom, 11 and there will be great earthquakes, and in various places plagues and famines; and there will be terrors and great signs from heaven.

MATTHEW 24:8 (MARK 13:8B)

But all these things are merely the beginning of birth pangs.

LUKE 21:12–24 (MARK 13:9)

But before all these things, they will lay their hands on you and will persecute you, delivering you to the synagogues and prisons, bringing you before kings and governors for My name's sake. 13 It will lead to an opportunity for your testimony. 14 So make up your minds not to prepare beforehand to defend yourselves; 15 for I will give you utterance and wisdom which none of your opponents will be able to resist or refute. 16 But you will be betrayed even by parents and brothers and relatives and friends, and they will put some of you to death, 17 and you will be hated by all because of My name. 18 Yet not a hair of your head will perish. 19 By your endurance you will gain your lives. 20 But when you see Jerusalem surrounded by armies, then recognize that her desolation is near. 21 Then those who are in Judea must flee to the mountains, and those who are in the midst of the city must leave, and those who are in the country must not enter the city; 22 because these are days of vengeance, so that all things which are written will be fulfilled. 23 Woe to those who are pregnant and to those who are nursing babies in those days; for there will be great distress upon the land and wrath to this people; 24 and they will fall by the edge of the sword, and will be led captive into all the nations; and Jerusalem will be trampled under foot by the Gentiles until the times of the Gentiles are fulfilled.

MATTHEW 24:9

Then they will deliver you to tribulation, and will kill you, and you will be hated by all nations because of My name.

MARK 13:11–13 (MATTHEW 24:10)

When they arrest you and hand you over, do not worry beforehand about what you are to say, but say whatever is given you in that hour; for it is not you who speak, but it is the Holy Spirit. 12 Brother will betray brother to death, and a father his child; and children will rise up against parents and have them put to death. 13 You will be hated by all because of My name, but the one who endures to the end, he will be saved.

MATTHEW 24:11–29 (MARK 13:10, 14–25, LUKE 21:25A)

Many false prophets will arise and will mislead many. 12 Because lawlessness is increased, most people's love will grow cold. 13 But the one who endures to the end, he will be saved. 14 This gospel of the kingdom shall be preached in the whole world as a testimony to all the nations, and then the end will come. 15 Therefore when you see the ABOMINATION OF DESOLATION which was spoken of through Daniel the prophet, standing in the holy place (let the reader understand), 16 then those who are in Judea must flee to the mountains. 17 Whoever is on the housetop must not go down to get the things out that are in his house. 18 Whoever is in the field must not turn back to get his cloak. 19 But woe to those who are pregnant and to those who are nursing babies in those days! 20 But pray that your flight will not be in the winter, or on a Sabbath. 21 For then there will be a great tribulation, such as has not occurred since the beginning of the world until now, nor ever will. 22 Unless those days had been cut short, no life would have been saved; but for the sake of the elect those days will be cut short. 23 Then if anyone says to you, 'Behold, here is the Christ,' or 'There He is,' do not believe him. 24 For false Christs and false prophets will arise and will show great signs and wonders, so as to mislead, if possible, even the elect. 25 Behold, I have told you in advance. 26 So if they say to you, 'Behold, He is in the wilderness,' do not go out, or, 'Behold, He is in the inner rooms,' do not believe them. 27 For just as the lightning comes from the east and flashes even to the west, so will the coming of the Son of Man be. 28 Wherever the corpse is, there the vultures will gather. 29 But immediately after the tribulation of those days THE SUN WILL BE DARKENED, AND THE MOON WILL NOT GIVE ITS LIGHT, AND THE STARS WILL FALL from the sky, and the powers of the heavens will be shaken.

LUKE 21:25B–26

And on the earth dismay among nations, in perplexity at the roaring of the sea and the waves, 26 men fainting from fear and the expectation of the things which are coming upon the world; for the powers of the heavens will be shaken.

MATTHEW 24:30 (MARK 13:26, LUKE 21:27)

And then the sign of the Son of Man will appear in the sky, and then all the tribes of the earth will mourn, and they will see the SON OF MAN COMING ON THE CLOUDS OF THE SKY with power and great glory.

LUKE 21:28

But when these things begin to take place, straighten up and lift up your heads, because your redemption is drawing near.

MATTHEW 24:31-35 (MARK 13:27-31, LUKE 21:29-33)

And He will send forth His angels with A GREAT TRUMPET and THEY WILL GATHER TOGETHER His elect from the four winds, from one end of the sky to the other. 32 Now learn the parable from the fig tree: when its branch has already become tender and puts forth its leaves, you know that summer is near; 33 so, you too, when you see all these things, recognize that He is near, right at the door. 34 Truly I say to you, this[16] generation will not pass away until all these things take place. 35 Heaven and earth will pass away, but My words will not pass away.

LUKE 21:34-36

Be on guard, so that your hearts will not be weighted down with dissipation and drunkenness and the worries of life, and that day will not come on you suddenly like a trap; 35 for it will come upon all those who dwell on the face of all the earth. 36 But keep on the alert at all times, praying that you may have strength to escape all these things that are about to take place, and to stand before the Son of Man.

---

16   (Matthew 24:34) The Greek word *houtos* translated here as "this" can also be translated as "that," indicating that Jesus was not necessarily talking about the generation of people hearing him speak. Rather, "that" generation which at some unspecified point in the future would see the beginning of events leading up to His return would not all die before it was fulfilled. The same Greek word is translated "this" in the parallel passages concerning Jesus' Second Coming in Mark (13:30) and Luke (21:32). However, as if to emphasize that a future generation and not his immediate audience would indeed see his return, Jesus used a different word translated "this" in Matthew 23:36. In that passage Jesus had been condemning the murderous hypocrisy of the Pharisees who were hearing Him, and He called upon them the blood of the righteous men they and their predecessors had killed. He said, "All these things shall come upon this generation." In this instance the Greek word *taute* is translated "this." *Taute* has the single meaning "this one." In other words, people living at that time (likely including some or all of His hearers) would see God's punishment for their sin. That punishment occurred in 70 A.D. when the Romans destroyed Jerusalem including the Temple. If Jesus had meant to say in the passages that clearly speak of His Second Coming that the generation hearing Him would see His coming in "the clouds of heaven," Matthew, Mark, and Luke would have used *taute*, a word that would have removed all doubt. The usual explanation of the passage assumes the translation of *genea* to be the alternative "race," rather than "generation," which would mean that the Jewish people would continue to exist until Christ returns. Either understanding destroys the argument of skeptics that Jesus was mistaken about when He would return and therefore could not be God.

MARK 13:34-37

It is like a man away on a journey, who upon leaving his house and putting his slaves in charge, assigning to each one his task, also commanded the doorkeeper to stay on the alert. 35 Therefore, be on the alert—for you do not know when the master of the house is coming, whether in the evening, at midnight, or when the rooster crows, or in the morning— 36 in case he should come suddenly and find you asleep. 37 What I say to you I say to all, 'Be on the alert!'

MATTHEW 24:36-42 (MARK 13:32-33)

But of that day and hour no one knows, not even the angels of heaven, nor the Son, but the Father alone. 37 For the coming of the Son of Man will be just like the days of Noah. 38 For as in those days before the flood they were eating and drinking, marrying and giving in marriage, until the day that Noah entered the ark, 39 and they did not understand until the flood came and took them all away; so will the coming of the Son of Man be. 40 Then there will be two men in the field; one will be taken and one will be left. 41 Two women will be grinding at the mill; one will be taken and one will be left. 42 Therefore be on the alert, for you do not know which day your Lord is coming."[17]

---

17   (Matthew 24:42) Although we cannot know the day and hour of Jesus' Second Coming, God is not the author of confusion, so there should be none concerning this important doctrine. According to conservative Bible scholars, scripture is to be understood first in its simplest, most straightforward meaning in its immediate context. Other passages that relate to the verses being studied can and should be used to help interpret the passage in question. In addition to Matthew 24, other scriptures dealing with Christ's return that, according to some Bible teachers, help reveal the order of events preceding it include Daniel 9-12, Joel 2-3, I Thessalonians 4-5, II Thessalonians 2, and, of course, Revelation, as well as others. Care should be taken not to let words be defined or passages be interpreted by scholars or teachers when those interpretations or definitions are not clearly supported by scripture.

Chapter 6
What is the Significance?

We have seen that rather than being in conflict with and contradicting one another, the Gospels actually are reliable witnesses to these and other events in the life of Jesus Christ. But why is it so important that they aren't really in conflict but rather are actually telling different parts of the same story? In my opinion it is significant because it is just one additional piece of evidence indicating that not just the Gospels but, in fact, the entire Bible is the inerrant Word of God. If the Gospels are not accurate in what they relate, then how do we determine if any part of the Bible is to be trusted? Each Gospel writer individually is accurate in what he recorded. But in order to see a more complete picture, the details of two, three, or all four must be blended together where it is appropriate to do so. When the Gospel accounts are read together at such points, the supposed discrepancies disappear and the authority of the Bible is demonstrated to be sure.

However, due to the lack of a complete presentation of Jesus' entire life and ministry, not every event recorded in more than one of the Gospels can be reconciled, even when they appear on the surface to be the same. If similar accounts in more than one Gospel differ in detail, it may be the result of their being the records of different occasions when Jesus repeated the same teaching or performed the same type of miracle, or it could be the result of their actually being the accounts of a single event or teaching recorded from different eyewitness perspectives, such as the events and teachings that are the focus of this book.

The Gospels certainly reveal that, although He was a Man, Jesus was not just an ordinary man. But if Jesus was not an ordinary human being like all others before and since, how was He different? What does the Bible say about Him? What did He say about Himself? It is clear from the historical record, including non-biblical sources, that He was a human being. He lived, felt emotion, suffered physical pain, and died. But it is equally clear from history that that was not all. The four Gospels, as well as secular historians of the time, agree in saying that Jesus did not remain dead. Who then was He?

John 1:1–4 says this about Jesus: "In the beginning was the Word, and the Word was with God, and the Word was God. He was in the beginning with God. All things came into being through Him, and apart from Him nothing came into being that has come into being. In Him was life, and the life was the Light of men."

JESUS IS GOD

Inspired by God, John states in this passage one of the foundational doctrines of historical Biblical Christianity: that Jesus (the Word) is God. He was not just a man—a created being—and, therefore, He was not merely a good man, a great teacher, or a prophet. Rather, being God the Son, He has always existed. In John 10:30 Jesus states unequivocally, "I and the Father are one." This single statement alone makes it impossible to say, as many critics have claimed, that Jesus did not believe that He was God. But there are additional statements by Jesus recorded in scripture as well, such as Matthew 7:21, Luke 22:28–30, and John 10:38, 14:9, 17:11, 21.

Jesus is the second Person of the Trinity: the Father, the Son, and the Holy Spirit. He is fully, truly God and fully, truly Man in one Person. Although He became a Man, He made His claim to be God perfectly understandable by the above statement. In fact, it was for that admission that the Jewish leaders tried unsuccessfully to stone Jesus (John 10:31). But it was His agreeing with the religious leaders' charge of claiming to be the "the Christ, the Son of God" (Matthew 26:63; see also Mark 14:61, Luke 22:70) during His trial for which they sought to have Him killed by the Romans. In their eyes, for Him to confess that He was the Son of God made Jesus guilty of the blasphemy of assuming equality with God, which was punishable under Jewish law by death.

Knowing that by making this claim Jesus would assure His own execution, there could be only two possible reasons He would do so. Either Jesus was insane, believing Himself to be God when He was not, or He was actually who He said He was—God, who had for some purpose become a Man. If the first reason for His claim to be God was correct, then all of Jesus' disciples would likewise have had to be mentally ill, or at least deluded, to continue to believe in Him after His death. But hundreds of people could not all have the same hallucination, all seeing at one time a man who had come back to life after having witnessed his death. Some skeptics have proposed that Jesus was simply lying about His being God. But for a man to continue to lie when to do so would mean being tortured to death would seem to indicate some form of mental illness if not insanity.

If the second reason was true—if He was in fact God—then there should be some evidence of His divinity. If God had entered the world as a human being, it would seem logical that there would be unusual circumstances surrounding the event. Bringing men from opposite ends of the social order (the magi were wealthy and respected whereas shepherds were filthy outcasts) within perhaps days of each other, and possibly even from opposite ends of a vast continent, to worship a baby born to a virgin would certainly qualify as unusual.

In addition, His birth was announced, and His mother and stepfather were given instructions and warnings by angels. The magi followed an unusual star that moved before them, only stopping when it came to rest over Jesus' birthplace. Jesus' birth fulfilled prophecies recorded in the Old Testament hundreds of years earlier, prophecies which, were He only a man, would have been impossible for Him to bring about as an unborn baby in his mother's womb. How could he have simply manipulated world events in order that His place of birth would fulfill a prophecy made centuries before by the prophet Micah (Micah 5:2)? How could He, again, were He just a man, have caused Himself to be born to a woman who was a virgin and a descendant of King David so that He would be called the son (or descendant) of David himself? Only if He was God could these things have been done.

No ordinary man could have performed such wonderful miracles as Jesus did during his adult life. But the greatest and most unarguable evidence for His divinity came ultimately in the fact that the Jewish leaders could not produce Jesus' body after His disciples proclaimed in the streets of Jerusalem that He had risen from the dead. His death was a fact verified by the Roman soldiers responsible for His crucifixion. They, of all people, knew from much personal experience how to determine if a man was dead. After all, killing was their business. In that day and time before modern medicine, it is likely that any of the wounds and resulting blood loss Jesus suffered during his scourging and crucifixion would have been enough to kill Him, even if He had not remained on the cross to the point of death, if not from shock then certainly from infection. But Jesus suffered those wounds during His slow execution, and just to be sure, even though it was evident that Jesus was already dead, a soldier pierced His side.

In a preemptive effort to silence Jesus' disciples, the chief priests were forced to bribe the Roman soldiers, who had witnessed the resurrection, to tell the lie that His followers had come and stolen his body during the night while the soldiers were asleep (Matthew 28:11–15). Although we do not know the fate of those Roman soldiers for their failure to carry out their mission (normally punished by death), the one thing we do know is that the chief priests did not have Jesus' body with which to discredit His disciples. It is very likely that the Jewish leaders had been to Jesus' tomb and knew that His body was in fact missing. For that reason they tried to silence the guards with money.[18] That is significant evidence for the resurrection.

---

18   Compiled by Bill Wilson, *The Best of Josh McDowell: A Ready Defense* (Thomas Nelson, 1993) 234–235.

Jesus' followers went from hiding in fear of also being put to death to boldly and publicly preaching that He was alive again. They could never have been led out of hiding by a mere spiritual appearance or by a man barely alive who, instead of dying on a cross from extreme trauma, had somehow overcome physical shock in the cool tomb three days after a failed crucifixion and been rescued by a well-armed group of trained soldiers (which Jesus did not have). The fact is that being in a cool tomb would actually have caused him to die more quickly from shock if He had still been alive when He was placed there (though we know He was not). But granting for the sake of argument the possibility of that absurd idea, Jesus would have been in desperate need of immediate emergency medical care in order to survive. However, such care would not exist for nearly two thousand years. A man in that condition having been rescued from death by his followers could not have inspired them to continue telling the lie of his physical resurrection from death for no reward other than their own deaths as martyrs. No, the radical change in the behavior of Jesus' disciples has no explanation outside of the reality of Jesus' physical resurrection from death!

Jesus was actually God as He claimed to be and did just what He predicted that He would do by returning to life and appearing to His followers, although in a physical body that would never again die and that was not subject to the physical laws of nature. For instance, He appeared among the disciples while they were in a locked room. Solid walls and barred doors couldn't keep Him out! He disappeared after the disciples on the road to Emmaus recognized Him. The fact that His resurrection was physical and not merely spiritual was proved by His eating food in their presence on several occasions. His disciples could touch Him and see the terrible scars of His torture. He was able to do these things because, in addition to being a Man, Jesus was and is God.

JESUS IS CREATOR

The second aspect of Jesus' identity, as we are told in John 1:1 and other passages (I Corinthians 8:6, Colossians 1:16, and others), is that He is the very one by Whom and for Whom the entire universe was created. Genesis 1:1 says, "In the beginning God created the heavens and the earth." This stands in direct opposition to what a majority of, but by no means all, scientists claim to be the "uncontestable fact" of the evolution of life from non-living chemicals hundreds of millions of years ago on a primitive earth that was very unlike the earth of today. So, did the universe and all life come into being all by themselves, which is what evolution demands, or did God create it from nothing?

While seemingly ignoring the fact that life comes only from life and never from non-living matter (experimentally tested and proven in the nineteenth century by Louis Pasteur), evolutionists claim that their theory is undeniable and that life somehow sprang from non-living chemicals at least once in the distant past. But rather than being a tested and proven scientific fact, evolution is actually impossible to test, as is creation for that matter, and can neither be verified nor falsified by scientific experimentation.[19]

---

19   John Chaikowski, "Geology v. Physics," Geotimes, 50 (April 2005): 165, quoted in Creation: *The Journal of the Creation Science Movement* 14(September 2005): 15, <https://www.csm.org.uk/journals/2005-4.pdf?PHPSESSID=donjmkalr>.

Therefore, evolution does not even qualify for the title "theory" in the classical definition of the term. It is merely a philosophy or a way of looking at and thinking about the world and its origins. Both evolution and creation are in reality conflicting worldviews. They are positions held by faith by their respective adherents.[20] For that reason they are both equally religious interpretations of past events, one atheistic and the other theistic. But they are also equally scientific models used to explain the data. Knowing that, the question then becomes one of which interpretation or model best fits the observable facts and explains what we see in nature without confusion and self-contradiction.

Fields of science that deal with discovering the origin and history of the earth and universe, such as astronomy, archaeology, and historical geology, are known as historical science, whereas other areas of science, such as chemistry, biology, physics, the remaining sub-fields of geology, and the applied-science field of engineering, all of which utilize and advance knowledge and technology, are often described as operational science. Historical science attempts to understand how certain events occurred once in the unobserved past, whereas operational science investigates and observes matter and processes that exist and operate in the present. But, unknown to most laymen, there is a great difference between the two. In attempting to piece together the origin and history of the universe, the earth, and life, historical scientists can only look at the things around them: the planets, stars, galaxies, rocks, fossils, and the incredibly complex living organisms that live on the earth.

---

[20] L. Harrison Matthews in *The Origin of Species* by Charles Darwin (London: J. M. Dent and Sons, Ltd., 1971) x.

However, in order to explain how and when all matter and life came into existence and how the earth came to look the way it does, all of the data collected or described in the field must be thoroughly examined. But then, since there is no one living now who was there in the distant past to witness how the things observed came to exist, the facts must be interpreted. The attempt to reconstruct earth's geologic and biological history is the single goal of historical science. But, it is actually the interpretation of the data, not the data itself, which is the very essence of this reconstruction and is the actual basis of the creation versus evolution debate.

Operational science also begins with observation of the physical world, but the observations are then followed by experimental testing that either verifies (proves) or falsifies (disproves) the hypotheses that come from the observations. This is what is known as the scientific method, and it was this scientific method that led to the discovery of the laws of science themselves. The contrast between the historical and operational methods is clear. Operational science equals observation of facts followed by scientific experimentation, whereas historical science equals observation of facts followed only by interpretation of those facts by the observer.

What most secular scientists refuse to admit, at least in public, and what almost all non-scientists have never heard is that the process of interpretation is, by its very nature, subject to the personal prejudices or biases of the scientific observer. A perfect example of this truth is found, not in science, but in a court room. Scientific examples will be discussed later. In a trial, there is a standard cast of characters consisting of a prosecuting attorney, a defense attorney, a defendant, a judge, and a jury. Both attorneys have all of the facts bearing on the case. The prosecutor has spent many hours examining those facts and has pieced together a story of the events surrounding the crime, which occurred in the unobserved past. His story shows that the defendant is guilty beyond reasonable doubt. Unfortunately for the prosecutor, but to the delight of the accused, the defense attorney has examined the exact same facts but has developed a totally different story, one that shows that his client is innocent, or at least that there is a reasonable doubt as to his guilt.

The attorney that "proves the truth" of his story wins the case. But in the legal sense, "prove" means only that after convincing himself, the attorney has also convinced the twelve members of the jury that his interpretation of the facts—his story about the past—is the correct one and that it is "true." The question is how two convincing yet totally contradicting stories could spring from the same body of facts in the first place. The answer is that the two lawyers are biased. The defense attorney assumes the innocence of the defendant whereas the prosecutor assumes his guilt. It is these opposing biases, or assumptions, held by the attorneys long before the facts are examined that result in their conflicting interpretations. Ironically, the fact that one lawyer "proves" that his story of past events is true does not necessarily mean that it is actually true. It may mean that one interpretation of the facts was more convincing than the other or simply that one attorney was a better storyteller.

The same is true in historical science. Andrew A. Snelling, Ph.D., a creationist geologist, has distinguished between the terms "data" and "evidence" even though the two words are normally used to mean the same thing. In the context of geology, "data" refers to the repeatable measurements and observations made in the field by looking at the rocks. Examples of such data would be descriptions of the shape and mineralogy of grains in sandstone, folds in rock layers, or fossils that may be present. "Data" becomes "evidence" that can be used to support one side of a discussion about the origin of the rocks or fossils when the data is interpreted.[21] Scientific data collected in the field corresponds with the facts that are interpreted and used in the legal arguments. Again, as in the trial, the field observations are turned into evidence through the process of interpretation. It is the interpretation by the scientist that is intended to persuade the opinion of others.

Just as with the attorneys, what scientists believe about the past (their bias) before beginning their investigations predetermines how they will interpret the data that, again, only exists in the present. The existence of this bias or prejudice and its control over interpretation is the most closely guarded secret of the evolutionistic historical scientific fraternity. Their bias is so engrained that many, if not all, evolutionists fail to see that they are biased. Like a good trial lawyer, a successful evolutionist must have a talent for creating a believable interpretation of the observations and presenting that interpretation in a convincing manner, especially when it contradicts other established evolutionists. If nothing else, evolutionists must be good storytellers.

Dr. Mary Schweitzer turned the science of paleontology (the science of the study of fossils) on its head when she discovered soft tissue and blood vessels containing apparent red blood cells

---

21   Andrew A. Snelling, *Earth's Catastrophic Past: Geology, Creation and the Flood, Volume 1* (Dallas, TX: Institute for Creation Research, 2009) 295.

in fossil dinosaur bones.[22] But she really didn't mean to do that. Like many other important discoveries throughout the history of science, it sort of happened by accident. She noticed that some fossil dinosaur bones smelled like dead tissue not like bone that had been replaced by silica or some other mineral during fossilization. Because of her biology background that odor led her to investigate the cause.

When she saw under her microscope what appeared to be transparent blood vessels containing red blood cells that a graduate lab assistant found she couldn't believe it. Her evolutionary bias instantly took over. "My colleague brought it back and showed me, and I just got goose bumps, because everyone knows these things don't last for 65 million years."[23] Interestingly, her initial reaction was the same as that of pretty much all other paleontologists. They are aware that, if nothing else, radiation would destroy the soft tissue.

Many in her field initially criticized her saying that she had not been thorough in her methods. She had published her first peer reviewed journal article without as much data as she would have liked, but realized that grant money would not have been available to continue her research if she didn't publish. It seems that money and professional prestige contribute to the bias of scientists. But Dr. Schweitzer received her grants, and her research yielded more and more soft tissue.

Others finally stopped criticizing and began to look for soft tissue in fossils that were only partially replaced by minerals,

---
22   Barry Yeoman Journalist "Schweitzer's Dangerous Discovery" Originally published in *Discover*, April 2006 *http://www.barryyeoman.com/articles/schweitzer.html*, Accessed September 2010.
23   Ibid.

verifying her findings. But in spite of the fact that she and most other paleontologists first believed that "these things don't last for 65 million years" Dr. Schweitzer is now seen as the pioneer of a new field of science that looks for biomolecules – the molecules of life – in fossils in the attempt to piece together the evolution of all living things from non-living chemicals. Their bias prevents them from even considering the alternative, that the only partially mineralized fossils containing soft original organic tissue are not 65 million years old – that they are only about 4,500 years old and are the result of the Genesis Flood which destroyed most of the life that God had created. It seems that an entirely new career choice has sprung up from the fertile ground of evolutionary bias because Dr. Schweitzer is such a good story teller about the unobserved past.

Unknown to most people, the very definition of "science" itself has been dramatically changed to reflect this prejudice that evolutionists deny. "Science" used to mean something like "the examination of the world by the use of observation and repeatable experimentation." The definition now is, in condensed form, "the search for a naturalistic, materialistic explanation for the universe and everything in it including life." In other words, they are looking for any explanation for the universe and life that involves only natural processes acting on matter. But what they really want is an explanation for the universe that denies the reality of God. Creationist science is, therefore, excluded from "science" by definition.

It's no wonder, then, that secular scientists, who tend to be agnostics or atheists, see the evidence as "proving" evolution to be true. It "proves" evolution because they want it to. Like an attorney, they have convinced themselves their story is true. They do not want to face the possibility of the existence of a transcendent, personal God to whom they must be accountable. The fact is, they really just don't want to give up their sin, and believing in evolution gives them the justification to hold on to it. Again, like the attorney, they attempt to convince those who hear them that their interpretation of the evidence, their story about the past, is true.

Scientists who are Christians and take the Bible, including Genesis, seriously—and there are thousands of scientists around the world who are young-earth creationists, most of whom hold earned Ph.D.s from major secular universities—see the evidence as confirming the biblical account of the Creation of the universe, earth, and life and earth's subsequent destruction by a global flood. They do so because they understand that God is who He claims to be and that the Bible, being a true eyewitness account of earth's actual history, is His authoritative written Word. Therefore, every aspect of life, including scientific investigation, is to be grounded in it and guided by it.

A third group of scientists attempts to fit billions of years of earth history and evolution into the Bible. They refer to themselves as "theistic evolutionists," "progressive creationists," or other such names but still are mostly evolutionists although most or all claim to be Christians. All scientists, evolutionists and creationists alike, are indeed biased before they even begin. Just in looking primarily at two areas of science, biology and geology, we can easily see how presuppositions or assumptions about the past control the historical scientific interpretation of the observed facts.

Due to their bias, biologists who are young-earth creationists hold to a literal, recent Creation of life by God as recorded in Genesis and recognize signs of His creative design in all living things no matter their degree of complexity. Generally, the term "complexity" in the evolutionistic sense relates merely to the size of the organism in question with small organisms being "simple." But even bacteria, the smallest truly living organisms, are incredibly complex (viruses are smaller but are not living organisms since they do not reproduce; they invade healthy cells and use the cells' machinery to duplicate themselves). Some of these "simple" bacteria have molecular motors connected to a tiny hair or cilia that turn at thousands of revolutions per minute to provide mobility. Each cell in every living organism has within it complex molecular factories and transport systems that bring into the cell raw materials, manufacture and carry from place to place within the cell the proteins and enzymes needed for life, and remove waste products. The so-called "simple" cell is anything but simple since it contains all of the components of a large city but on a molecular scale. These molecular motors, factories, and transport systems, as well as all organ-level and system-level tissues in plants, animals, and humans, are made of interrelated parts that all have to function together. Michael Behe (1996), in his book *Darwin's Black Box*, coined the term "irreducible complexity"[24] to describe such systems.

The concept of irreducible complexity means that these intricate systems could not have evolved piece by piece since the individual parts would have no function without the others all in place and complete. As a result, any newly evolved part of

---

24   Michael J, Behe, 2006, Darwin's Black Box, New York, NY, Free Press, p. 39.

a cell, organ, or system randomly evolved in isolation would not give the organism an advantage that would help it survive. Instead, the supposed beneficial genetic copying errors, or mutations, that are assumed to produce the incomplete change would cause the organism to be less able to survive to maturity. Any resulting non-functional, partially evolved organ or system actually would hinder its owner's survival since it would use precious energy while returning nothing. As a result, the incomplete evolving system, as well as the supposed new DNA causing it, would not be passed to the next generation by way of natural selection since there would not be a next generation for the unfortunate plant or animal. The complete and complex systems we see in living organisms must have been present from the very beginning in order to function. For example, what good is a heart with no blood, blood vessels, lungs, or a complex brain and nervous system to coordinate its function? The same question can be asked about every part of every system in every living organism.

Since no naturalistic mechanism (as we will see, mutations are not a good candidate) can explain the gradual rise of irreducibly complex structures in living organisms, both the organisms and the tissues and systems that make them up must have first originated fully formed, which is the long way of saying they must have been created. Even so, evolutionists see these complex systems and assume that they arose by chance mutation over vast eons of time. This assumption is the result of their atheistic bias and is held without even a shred of scientific proof that it is true. Remember, there are only observable facts that must be interpreted through the "filter" of the observer's bias.

In addition to a living cell's structural complexity, the DNA in its nucleus contains information equal to that contained in hundreds of volumes of reference books.[25] The information on this page is not the result of inherent properties of the ink and paper. Written information comes only from intelligence that has the ability to arrange the ink on the paper so that it makes sense to a reader who also must have equal intelligence with which to decode and understand it. As in the case of written words, the information in DNA is not due to the properties of the matter of which it is composed. It too must come from intelligence. Evolution demands that random mutations must cause genetic information to increase over time, but that has never been seen to occur. Accidents (genetic mutations are copying errors or accidents) only destroy information and order.

Although there is a small number of genetic mutations that seem to give a "beneficial" effect to their carriers, such as sickle cell trait in some African tribes, the benefit usually comes at a cost to the long-term survivability of the organism. People having sickle cell trait, a genetic blood disorder causing resistance to malaria, tend to die early from sickle cell rather than malaria. Even so, these so-called "positive mutations" are held up as examples of evolution. All mutations, even the "beneficial" ones, result in a loss of genetic information and are discovered only by the often fatal diseases or deformities that they cause in the organism. Irreducible complexity in living systems and molecular information in DNA cannot be the result of chance

---

25   Carl Wieland, "The marvelous 'message molecule,'" *Creation* 4, 17 (September 1995):10-13.

accidental mutations that destroy information. Only the Creation of the earth and all the living organisms on it by God can adequately explain the presence and astounding diversity of life.

Evolutionists show their bias against this evidence for design and information in living organisms by merely attributing it all to the nature of matter. In spite of the scientific evidence to the contrary, matter must somehow have the ability to organize itself so that it appears to have been designed and contain information without intelligent input. Their reason? Because their prior assumption that there is no God demands that Creation cannot be true.

According to evolutionists, life supposedly first arose on the primitive earth when non-living chemicals in a hot, salty ocean somehow organized themselves into a molecule that could copy itself. These scientists are presented at this point with a difficult problem in their thought experiments (the only "experiments" they have) from which they develop their idea—their story—of how life first sprang into being. This idea is known as "chemical evolution." They say that life somehow began in water even though they fail to realize that water destroys DNA and its chemical precursors.[26] Heat and salt would only increase the water's destructiveness. Even though they imagine this watery origin of DNA, they also insist that there could have been no free oxygen in the earth's atmosphere because they *do* recognize the destructiveness of oxygen to amino acids and proteins as well as the molecules from which DNA is made.

---

26   "Knowing toil, knowing soil," Creation Ministries International, <http://creation.com/knowing-toil-knowing-soil> (accessed 2008).

But if water were present, then free oxygen would also have been present in the atmosphere because some molecules of water in the vapor state will split apart naturally to form hydrogen and oxygen gases.[27] However, if, as evolutionists believe, there had been no oxygen to combine with hydrogen, then there could have been no water in which the DNA could form—if DNA could form in water. But on the other hand, if there had been no destructive free oxygen to form destructive water, there would have been no beneficial ozone layer in the upper atmosphere to protect the evolving life from the sun's ultraviolet light, which is also very destructive to organic molecules.[19 28] "Life" would have been destroyed faster than it could have evolved!

But all of this discussion about water and oxygen does not address yet another basic problem for the notion of chemical evolution. That problem is the fact that DNA is not self-copying. All living cells that contain a nucleus and DNA have molecular machinery of astounding multiple-step complexity that accurately copies their genetic code. The same would have to have been true for any supposed ancient precursor to DNA. It could not have just assembled itself from a watery chemical "soup" as the evolutionist's story goes. Evolution cannot explain how this complicated duplicating system, which requires the existence of a living cell and is actually self-correcting, but which on rare occasion still makes copying errors, could have appeared by chance as a result of those errors.

---

27   Jonathan Sarfati, "15 loopholes in the evolutionary theory of the origin of life: Summary," Creation Ministries International, <http://creation.com/loopholes-in-the-evolutionary-theory-of-the-origin-of-life-summary> (accessed 2008).

28   Ibid.

What exactly then were the conditions on earth when life supposedly first appeared on its own? Was there water? Was there no oxygen? Was there both, or neither? The geologic record, containing rocks such as limestone (a rock made of carbon plus oxygen) and minerals like hematite (iron plus oxygen) in the oldest or deepest sediments,[29] settles the issue in that it shows that there has always been free oxygen present in the earth's atmosphere, just as there has always been water in which the sediments were deposited. So what is a poor evolutionist to do with that information? He does what he always does when the scientific facts confuse his explanation (his story) of unobserved history. He steps around the facts and forges ahead in his willfully ignorant and often self-contradictory interpretation of those facts, blind to the truth that, due to his bias, he has sacrificed scientific objectivity to his god of atheistic materialism, otherwise known as evolution.

But do all evolutionists always agree on their idea about origins and its significance? It is informative to hear what the evolutionists themselves say about the importance of evolution to scientific disciplines such as biology, which claims to have the truth about how life appeared. Certainly there must be unanimous opinion on this point. An anonymous article posted on the website for the evolutionist/atheist National Center for Science Education is a good place to start.[30] There it states, "The

---

29   "Deep sea rocks point to early oxygen on earth," Penn State Live, <http://live.psu.edu:80/story/38514> (accessed April 2009).

30   "Idaho Scientists for Quality Science Education," National Center for Science Education, 2000, <http://ncseweb.org/media/voices/idaho-scientists-quality-science-education> (accessed January 24, 2009).

Theory of Evolution ranks as one of the great discoveries in the intellectual history of science. Its impact on biology is analogous to that of Newton's law on physics, Copernicus' heliocentric (Sun-centered) theory of the universe on astronomy and the theory of plate tectonics on geology." A few paragraphs later it says, "Thus, evolution is the central organizing principle that biologists use to understand the natural world. As Time magazine (December 31, 1999) recently said, 'Yet Darwinism remains one of the most successful scientific theories ever promulgated. There is hardly an element of humanity ... certainly not biology—that can be fully understood without its help.'"

Those scientists sound pretty certain that evolution is foundational to science in general and biology in particular. But there are other evolutionists with a different opinion. Regarding the newly discovered fact that the majority of human DNA that does not code for proteins in the cell (so-called "junk DNA" that is supposedly left over from evolution) actually seems to function as a computer operating system for the genome and is not the useless residue of evolution it was assumed to be, Dr. John Mattick states, "'The failure to recognize the full implications of [non-protein-coding DNA] may well go down as one of the biggest mistakes in the history of molecular biology'"(brackets in original).[31] But how can a scientific idea coming from the assumption of evolution be a hindrance to science if evolution is so important? Perhaps it is not so important after all. Perhaps it

---

31   Jonathan Sarfati, "Electric DNA," Creation Ministries International (2007), <http://creation.com/electric-dna> (accessed January 24, 2009).

is just a made-up story about the unobserved past, a story that is based on the desire for there to be no God.

However, scientists who are young-earth creationists do not have such glaring internal self-contradictions concerning their interpretations of scientific facts. They look at the world very differently than do evolutionists. For instance, geologists who are young-earth creationists see the same sedimentary rock layers, the same lack of fossils of intermediate life forms (those are necessary if evolution is true), the same sedimentary rock layers containing gaps in the fossil sequence, the same fossil trees that cross several different rock layers representing hundreds of thousands of years in the geologic time scale, the same "fossil graveyards" containing billions of fossilized plants and animal bones, and other describable geologic data that evolutionists do. They see them but do not have to perform mental games like the evolutionists do in order to explain them. Such "anomalies" are actually the norm for evolutionary geologists and paleontologists as they continually have to revise their interpretation of earth's geologic and evolutionary history to make new facts fit. They have to keep changing their story.

For creationist geologists, these every-day "anomalies" are not anomalies at all. Rather, they are predicted by the catastrophic processes of the Flood portion of the Creation/Fall/Flood model of earth history as recorded in Genesis. Sedimentary sandstone rock layers interpreted by evolutionists as desert sand dune deposits reveal to creationists evidence of rapid deposition by deep, fast moving water. Such evidence is seen in large internal cross bed structures produced in underwater sand and fossil animal tracks that are only preserved in detail in sand that is water-saturated. Fine-grained sediments such as silt and clay that form mudstones have been shown to be laid down quickly by moving water rather than just settling at barely measurable rates out of quiet lakes,[32] which is the uniformitarian explanation. The term "uniformitarian" originally referred to those who believe that present assumed slow rates of sedimentation have been uniform over millions of years. However, that concept has begun to be revised in recent years to explain the increasing number of facts that demonstrate that most sedimentary rock layers are the result of catastrophic processes. This is known as "catastrophism," which says that most of the billions of years of geological time took place in the assumed gaps between the strata, which were deposited during violent events of short duration.[33] But in spite of the new acceptance of catastrophic processes to explain the rock strata, the old uniformitarian ideas still dominate the field of geology.

The normal idea of evolution demands that the process was very gradual with one life form changing bit by bit into another. The fact that there are no fossils of transitional or "in- between" life forms that are accepted without argument by evolutionary paleontologists is no problem for them. They merely assume that there are transitional fossils that have not yet been found. There must be such fossils because evolution is true. They "know" it is true because we all evolved. If that sounds rather odd, it is

---

[32] Tas Walker, "Mud experiments overturn long-held geologic beliefs," Creation Ministries International (2008), <http://creation.com/mud-experiments-overturn-long-held-geological-beliefs> (accessed January 24, 2009).

[33] Andrew A. Snelling, *Earth's Catastrophic Past: Geology, Creation and the Flood, Volume 2* (Dallas, TX: Institute for Creation Research, 2009) 486.

because it is. That type of thinking is called circular reasoning, which occurs when a scientist starts out by assuming the truth of the idea he is trying to prove. But, strange as it may seem, that is how evolutionists think.

The absence of transitional fossil evidence is not a problem for other more honest (but still mistaken) paleontologists because it has led to the development of a new model of how life evolved on the earth. This new model is called "punctuated equilibrium." This idea recognizes that there is no fossil evidence of gradual evolution and says that none will be found because life stayed the same without change over millions of years (the equilibrium part), forming all the fossils we find that show no significant change. All of the different species evolved in small areas of their populations in such quick jumps (the punctuated part) that no fossil evidence of it was preserved. It is very unusual for a complete lack of evidence to become the basis for a new scientific theory or model. It is also very unscientific. But such are the results of the atheistic bias that is the foundation of evolutionary thinking.

But, of course, creationist geologists see the absence of transitional forms as being exactly what the Flood-deposited sediments would preserve in the fossil record if there were no such transitional organisms to begin with. All living things were created and their fossils that are found in the rocks show essentially no change from present organisms. For creationists, there is no need to make up a story to explain the data that shows no change.

In most sedimentary rock outcrop locations around the world, the nearly flat and sharp contacts between rock layers supposedly represent millions of years of time during which there was no deposition occurring (the gaps of catastrophism). However, the contacts give every appearance of being continuous bedding planes between different strata or layers. In the Grand Canyon, one such contact is clearly shown to be a continuous deposition plane not representing a time gap at all. This occurs between the Esplanade Sandstone and the overlying Hermit Shale. The contact that is smooth and sharp in one place can be traced laterally to a point where the same two strata actually interfinger with each other, demonstrating that continuous deposition actually took place along the entire contact.[34] The same is true with contacts that seem to show evidence of slight erosion in one location (which is easily explained by characteristics of deep flowing water that would exist in a huge worldwide flood) but appear to be flat, continuous sedimentation planes in others.[35] What this means is that there is no real factual data that demands that there be gaps representing millions of years in the rock record.

In Yellowstone National Park, there is a well-known exposure of sedimentary rocks that contain fossilized trees, many of which are standing vertically, crossing various layers of sediments. Occasionally, vertical fossil trees are partially in coal and partially in other types of rock.[36] These tree fossils, known as polystrate

---

34   R. C. Blakey, "Stratigraphy and geologic history of Pennsylvanian and Permian rocks, Mogollon Rim region, central Arizona and vicinity," *Geological Society of America Bulletin*, 102:1205, cited in Andrew A. Snelling, *Earth's Catastrophic Past: Geology, Creation & the Flood, Volume 2* (Dallas, TX: Institute for Creation Research, 2009) 591.

35   Andrew A. Snelling, "The case of the 'missing' geologic time," Creation Ministries International (1992), <http://creation.com/the-case-of-the-missing-geologic-time> (accessed 2008).

36   Andrew A. Snelling, *Earth's Catastrophic Past: Geology, Creation & the Flood*, Volume 2 (Dallas, TX: Institute for Creation Research, 2009) 565.

fossils because they cross many (poly) layers (strata), are interpreted by evolutionists as representing ancient forests that were gradually buried over millions of years then fossilized. However, it's hard to imagine how a dead tree could survive for hundreds of thousands or millions of years without decaying to dust while it was being buried at the rate of a tiny fraction of an inch per year.

But, as with all geologic field data, that much time is not needed to explain them. A catastrophic global flood would explain fossil trees that cross multiple rock layers as having been deposited as they sank during a brief quiet period and then buried rapidly in a matter of minutes or hours by more rapidly moving, sediment-laden water.[37] The Flood of Genesis would also explain the presence of millions of fossils (fossil graveyards) of marine and land animals and plants buried and fossilized together in the same rock layers as is often the case. Plant and animals would be overwhelmed and their remains would be covered quickly in the sediment load being swept along by the deep, rapidly flowing flood waters.

A global flood and the unimaginably destructive forces that would have been associated with it would also explain such geological wonders as the unfractured hairpin folds frequently found in sedimentary rocks such as sandstone or shale. I saw many examples of smoothly folded rock layers during a summer geologic mapping college course in the western United States. These folds were obviously produced when the sediments slumped while they were still soft and water-saturated, although evolutionists say they

---

37 Jonathan Sarfati, "The Yellowstone petrified forests: Evidence of catastrophe," Creation Ministries International (1999), <http://creation.com/the-yellowstone-petrified-forests> (accessed May 2009).

formed slowly after hardening. Hard sedimentary rock does not bend far before breaking when stress is applied, even if the stress is applied gradually over hundreds or thousands of years. Geologists know that hard rock breaks because such breakage is represented by faults or fractures. Where faults are exposed, they show vertical movement of the hard rock layers on either side of the fracture rather than a gradual bending. Similar breakage would occur in the folds if the sedimentary rocks were hard when the folding happened. The sedimentary rocks all over the world that were folded before they hardened are consistent with the Genesis Flood.

While all of these lines of evidence are subject to the biases of interpretation mentioned earlier, occasionally new evidence is discovered that is so powerful that the theory it deals with would be totally discredited if the theory did not have to do with evolution and billions of years of time. One of the most foundational assumptions of evolutionary geology has been badly shaken by such new information. Evolutionary geologists insist that the geologic record we see all over the earth formed over billions of years, with the main basis for their assumption being the great ages measured by radioactive dating of certain types of rocks. This method of measuring the "age" of igneous rocks (formed from molten rock, or magma, deep within the earth at great temperatures and pressures or when magma comes to the surface through volcanoes) is based on the well-known process of decay of radioactive elements by nuclear fission to form stable non-radioactive elements. In reality, this procedure does not measure actual age. It measures the amounts of radioactive parent and stable daughter elements in the rock. The "age" of the rock is then calculated based on the known present rate of radioactive decay. Unfortunately for the evolutionists, radiometric dating doesn't seem to work very well since much new scientific data refutes its old-age claim.

Numerous volcanic rocks of historically known age have been tested using the potassium-argon (K-Ar) method. One lava flow in Hawaii, the Hualalai basalt, erupted from 1800 to 1801 but was "dated" using K-Ar as approximately 1.4 to 1.6 million years old. A lava flow from Sicily's Mt. Etna, which erupted in 1793, was dated as approximately 250,000 years old. There are many other such examples of radiometric "absolute dating" errors.[38]

A group of Ph.D. scientists with the Institute for Creation Research and the Creation Research Society have recently completed an eight-year research project, using the evolutionists' own testing methods and commercial testing laboratories, which has provided astounding evidence that the earth is not billions of years old. It seems that there is too much helium in zircon minerals in deep granitic rock for it to be 1.5 billion years old as dated by evolutionists.[39] Zircons contain uranium-238 which decays radioactively through eight steps to lead-206, with each step producing one helium atom as a byproduct.

Helium atoms do not combine with other chemical elements and, as a result, are free to move through the crystal structure of zircon. The creationist scientists collected tiny zircons from

---

[38] "More and more wrong dates: Radio-dating in Rubble," Creation Ministries International (2001), <http://creation.com/more-and-more-wrong-dates-radio-dating-in-rubble> (accessed 2007).

[39] Don DeYoung, Ph.D., *Thousands ... not Billions* (Master Books, 2005) 65–78.

the rock and sent them anonymously through a third party to a widely known expert to have the diffusion rate of the helium (the rate at which the helium atoms move through the crystal) measured precisely. The measured diffusion rate matched the curve that the creationists had predicted would be found before the test was conducted if the zircons, and therefore the granitic rock containing them, were only about 6,000 years old. Their prediction was in print before the results were received from the lab for verification of their theory!

Since there is present in the zircons evidence of sufficient radioactive decay to require hundreds of millions of years at present decay rates, the measurements require that the radioactive decay process that yielded the helium and lead was greatly accelerated at some point in the past, probably during the Flood year. The same research project discovered that both coal and diamonds still contain radioactive carbon-14, which should be completely gone after only about 50,000 to 60,000 years. But the coal samples tested were "dated" by evolutionist assumptions as being hundreds of millions of years old and the diamonds more than a billion. To make matters worse for the evolutionists, all of the coal samples that were tested had about the same amount of carbon-14 remaining, which indicates that the various coal beds were all deposited about the same time rather than hundreds of millions of years apart.

There is something wrong with the methodology of radiometric dating of rocks since it only "works" when the true historical age of the rock is unknown. It seems that it is not quite the death-blow to creation that the evolutionists think it is. Rather, their old-earth "clock" appears to be badly in need of repair. Or maybe it should be discarded altogether. In these cases, as in all others where "science" has "disproved" the Bible, particularly Genesis, the observed scientific facts are actually better explained by the Bible's historical account of the creation of the universe and all that it contains and the Flood which reshaped the earth's entire surface.

That is true even in my own career field of soil science. The majority of the soils in the Piedmont area of North Carolina (the area between the coastal plain and the mountains) where I was working supposedly formed over millions of years from weathered granitic or metamorphic rocks known as schist and gneiss. But after becoming a creationist in 1990, I began to notice for the first time that there were pieces of rounded gravel in these residual soils. The power of personal bias over the interpretation of observed data was demonstrated by the fact that I had always been able to see the gravel, but before becoming a creationist I simply overlooked it! The gravel was predominantly quartzite, a rock formed from sandstone by intense pressure and heat. But what made this observation shocking to me was four-fold.

First was the fact that being rounded meant that the gravel had been transported and deposited by water. Second was the fact that none of the assumed granite, schist, or gneiss parent rocks contain quartzite. Third was the fact that the gravel is often found in layers at the base of the soil and immediately over the actual weathered bedrock. Fourth was the fact that these soils with round gravel were on hilltops and side slopes, not just on stream flood plains where such round gravel would be expected.

It is an accepted fact of geology that any material that contains or overlies round gravel of any rock type is sedimentary except for the occasional basalt layer between sedimentary strata or flowing over the soil from volcanoes. That fact is reinforced when the gravel in soil is of a different rock type than the underlying bedrock. The gravelly material, the soil in this case, is where it is because it was brought there by the action of flowing water. As I traveled around the Piedmont region of North and South Carolina and Virginia, I looked for evidence of similar gravel. I found it essentially everywhere I looked. I began to search the scientific literature, both creationist and non-creationist, for reference to such gravels as those I was seeing. I was not surprised to find that soil scientists and geologists have been finding and describing similar gravels all over the world for many decades in the same ridge settings as I had found them.

Since evidence does not speak for itself and has to be interpreted, there were a couple of questions that had to be answered. What process or processes could deposit sediments containing rounded quartzite gravel over essentially the entire earth? Does the uniformitarian (or gradualistic) model or the catastrophic Genesis Flood model provide the most satisfactory explanation of the evidence?

The standard gradualistic explanation says that a nearly flat, slightly rolling eroded plain that gradually dropped below sea level and the ocean deposited sediments that covered it to a depth of hundreds or thousands of feet. After millions of years of uplift, the sediments were eroded away to the point we see today. The problem with that explanation is that it would predict that the present surface should cut across the stone layers more often than not. But what I have seen, and what is reported in the literature, is that wherever stone layers lie at the base of the soil, they are approximately parallel to the surface of the landscape.

The catastrophic Genesis Flood model would predict exactly what is seen all over the world. The intense power of the swiftly moving flood waters carved the nearly flat rolling piedmont plain and then covered it with more or less gravelly sediments as the water flowed off of the continents. The gravel carried in the sediments would be rounded quickly by the friction and pressure encountered during transport. As the water receded, it left a thin mantle of sediments with gravel layers often at the base of what would become the soil over the next thousand years or so.

As has been noted, evolutionists themselves are continually making new discoveries that defy a consistent scientific explanation within the evolution framework, causing them to repeatedly revise their story of the past. We have seen that in the examples of biology and geology, fields that are normally considered to be generally unrelated, established evolutionary interpretations of scientific data can be reinterpreted more satisfactorily and without self-contradiction when examined using the Creation/Flood model as a basis. In recent decades, there have been two widely studied catastrophic events, both involving volcanoes, which have caused evolutionists in both fields to stand back and wonder about what they thought they knew.

In 1963, the island of Surtsey was created near Iceland in a matter of weeks by the eruption of an undersea volcano from which lava continued to flow for several years. But geologists were astounded as they saw landforms such as sandy beaches, cliffs, lagoons, hollows, and glens develop literally within weeks on the new island. Evolutionary assumptions told these old-earth geologists that the rocks and landforms that had appeared on the island almost overnight should have required hundreds of thousands or millions of years to develop, and they found it hard to believe.[40] Likewise, the biologists who began visiting the island soon after the eruptions ceased were dumbfounded by the speed with which insects, plants, and birds began to populate the new island, and by the "wrong order" in which they appeared based on their assumptions about how life began and evolved on the earth.[41]

In 1980, Mount St. Helens erupted violently, reshaping the landscape and destroying the forests surrounding it in a matter of minutes. As with Surtsey, geologic features such as canyons and finely laminated sediments, both assumed to require at least hundreds of thousands of years, were formed within hours or days. Laboratory experiments have also demonstrated rapid laminate formation under moving water.[42] Again, as on Surtsey, the reestablishment of ecosystems on the devastated landscape began far sooner than evolutionists thought it could. In both locations, the new ecosystems that had arisen before their very eyes within years should have silenced their argument against the

---

40   Carl Wieland, "Surtsey, the young island that 'looks old,'" Creation Ministries International (1995), <http://creationontheweb.com/content/view/1745/> (accessed 2008).

41   David Catchpoole, "Surtsey still surprises," Creation Ministries International (2007), <http://creation.com/surtsey-still-surprises> (accessed April 2009).

42   Andrew Snelling, "Sedimentation Experiments: *Nature* finally catches up!" Creation Ministries International (1997), <http://creation.com/sedimentation-experiments-nature-finally-catches-up> (accessed May 2009).

Flood of Genesis that "mere" thousands of years were insufficient to establish mature symbiotic animal/vegetative communities and re-populate the earth with human beings after such a catastrophic event. However, the concept of "evolution as fact" lives on in their minds because they are blind to what the observable facts could otherwise tell them. But, thankfully, theirs is not the only scientific voice or view in spite of the fact that there are those who try to keep from public awareness all knowledge that there are Creationists doing real science.

If the popular media and atheist/evolutionist groups such as the so-called National Center for Science Education, whose stated purpose is to ensure that only evolution is taught in America's classrooms, are to be believed, only evolutionists can be real scientists (remember the revised definition of "science"). However, there are creationist Ph.D. scientists in essentially every scientific field from astronomy to zoology that are doing important scientific research every day—research that is impacting the lives of people all over the world. Few would know that Dr. Werner von Braun, who was instrumental in developing modern rocket science and who guided the American space program that placed men on the moon in the 1960s and 70s, became a Christian and a young-earth creationist.[43] Likewise, it is not widely known that Dr. Raymond Damadian, the inventor of magnetic resonance imaging (MRI) technology, is a Christian and a young-earth creationist and was denied the Nobel Prize for his work, apparently for his creationist stance.[44]

---

43   Ann Lamont, *21 Great Scientists Who Believed the Bible* (Australia: Creation Science Foundation, 1995) 242–251.

44   Carl Wieland, "The not-so-Nobel decision," *Creation* 26, 4 (September 2004):40-42.

These scientists and thousands more like them begin their scientific inquiries with the belief that the first eleven chapters of Genesis are historically and scientifically accurate. They believe that the universe, the earth, and all of life were created in a perfect state by Jesus Christ, but that world was destroyed by a global Flood as judgment for man's sinfulness. The evidence that comes from their science testifies to the truth of their biblical starting point because it testifies to the truth that Jesus is Creator.

JESUS IS LIFE

Since Genesis is the eyewitness account of the One who created the universe and therefore is true, it is significant that it says in 1:31 that the universe was created "very good." There was no death and suffering in the world until our great, great, great ... grandparents, Adam and Eve, sinned. If there had been millions of years of disease and death before Adam and Eve evolved or before they were created, both of which are beliefs held by many Christians, then God would have blessed disease and death as very good. But that is hardly consistent with the nature of God as described in his Word. The Bible tells us that the sin of Adam and Eve caused not only themselves but all of their descendants through Noah all the way to us to be separated from God. We have all inherited a sin nature, that is, a tendency always to sin given the choice to sin or not sin, from our parents and their parents all the way back to the garden of Eden.

Because we "all have sinned and fall short of the glory of God" (Romans 3:23), as a result we all will die since "the wages of sin is death" (Romans 6:23). Again, because of our sin, we all deserve to spend eternity apart from God in torment, initially in hell then, ultimately, in a place of infinite suffering and darkness (Matthew 8:12) called the lake of fire (Revelation 20:15). Tragically, most people who have ever lived will find themselves there forever (Matthew 7:13–14, 25:41–46).

However, God has prepared heaven as a place where there will no longer be death, sorrow, crying, or pain (Revelation 21:4) that will be the eternal home for the righteous (Matthew 25:31–40). The problem for mankind then becomes how to exchange our inherited sentence of eternal death, darkness, and punishment in the lake of fire for an eternity of life, light, and reward in the presence of God in heaven. What do we have to do to get to heaven instead of where we are headed from the moment of conception? No less an authority than Jesus, God the Son, tells us that we only have to be perfect just as God the Father is perfect (Matthew 5:48).

Perfection—that is, a life entirely without sin—is the standard we must meet to attain eternal life. On the surface, that seems to be a bit unfair of God. All that we have to be is the one thing that we cannot possibly be because of the sin nature we all have inherited from Adam. So how can we get from suffering to peace, from darkness to light, from death to life? Again, John 1:4 tell us, "In Him [Jesus the Messiah (Christ in Greek)] was life, and the life was the Light of men."

Isaiah 53 is the clearest presentation in the entire Old Testament of what the Messiah would do for His people. Jesus told the religious leaders to search the Scriptures (their Torah, or the Old Testament) because in them they thought they had eternal life, but those very scriptures testified about Jesus (John

5:39). He was likely referring to, among many other prophecies about Himself, Isaiah 53:6, which detailed beforehand that God would place upon the Messiah the sins of the entire world. That passage says, "All of us like sheep have gone astray, each of us has turned to his own way; but the LORD has caused the iniquity of us all to fall on Him." But how does this make us sinless so that we can enter heaven?

God spoke through Paul in II Corinthians 5:21 to tell us that "He made Him who knew no sin to be sin on our behalf, so that we might become the righteousness of God in Him." The phrase "who knew no sin" describes "Him," that is, Jesus, not us. Not only did Jesus, who was Himself sinless, receive our sins when He was on the cross, He somehow actually became our sins. At the same time, His righteousness or perfection became available for all who would confess that they are sinners and turn away from, or repent of, their sins and trust that He is God and that He died to pay their death sentence. Romans 5:8 says, "But God demonstrates His own love toward us, in that while we were yet sinners, Christ died for us." His death was sufficient to redeem all of mankind out of slavery to sin if we will only stop attempting to do it on our own by trying to "be good." But as stated above, repentance (which literally means changing your mind about sin) must precede salvation. Jesus said in Luke 13:5, "'I tell you, no, but unless you repent, you will all likewise perish.'" Repentance is stressed throughout the entire Bible as prerequisite to a relationship with God.

So it was actually an exchange—one of eternal proportions—that took place that day on a cross outside of Jerusalem: our sins for Jesus' perfect sinlessness, our darkness for His light, our death for His life. Purely by the grace (undeserved favor) and mercy of God toward us, He provided for us the only way to avoid hell and come into His presence in heaven. He did for us what we could never do for ourselves. Only by admitting that we are sinners unable to save ourselves and repenting (Luke 13:3), believing that Jesus was the perfect God-Man and placing our trust for eternal life in Jesus' sacrificial death for us on the cross rather than in our good deeds, can we receive the free gift of eternal life. Ephesians 2:8–9 tells us clearly that we cannot be good enough for heaven on our own: "For by grace you have been saved through faith; and that not of yourselves, it is the gift of God; not as a result of works, so that no one may boast."

But also key to the transaction is believing that God raised Jesus from the dead. Romans 10:9 says, "That if you confess with your mouth Jesus as Lord, and believe in your heart that God raised Him from the dead, you will be saved." If Jesus did not rise physically from the dead, then He was just an ordinary sinful man who had no authority to be the perfect sacrifice that would pay for our sins and satisfy God's righteousness. But we have seen that He was not ordinary. He is the Creator, the risen Son of God.

But how can we believe what the Bible says? After all, there are many "holy books" in existence. Every major religion has its own. We can believe it because the Bible claims to be the inspired Word of God and is unique in all of the world's religious writings in that it contains predictive prophecy. Along with all of the many hundreds of detailed prophecies which have already been fulfilled concerning Israel and the nations surrounding it,

Jesus Christ's miraculous birth, His divinity, and His death, burial, and resurrection were all written in the Old Testament centuries before he was born. Jesus fulfilled them all as the New Testament records. There is much evidence, both in the Bible and in the world around us, which makes having faith in Jesus as Creator and Redeemer, rather than being a blind faith in fables, a most reasonable and intellectually sound position.

It is the atheistic evolutionist, the one who believes there is nothing but dark oblivion after death, who must suspend rational thought to believe what is not merely a fable but a lie. That is, the lie that everything he sees, both living and non-living, somehow created itself from nothing and over billions of years evolved from chaos to its present order and complexity. He cannot learn the truth of how the universe came to be because truth cannot be learned. It can be revealed only by God because God alone is the source of all truth. But in a relativistic world most people ask as Pontius Pilate did, "'What is truth?'" (John 18:38).

The ultimate truth is that Jesus, God the Son and Creator of the universe, miraculously entered His creation as a human baby in order to buy mankind back, to redeem us from the wages of sin that are ours by birthright. Those wages that we deserve are eternal death and torment in hell and the lake of fire. Revelation 21:8 says, "But for the cowardly and unbelieving and abominable and murderers and immoral persons and sorcerers and idolaters and all liars, their part will be in the lake that burns with fire and brimstone, which is the second death." Jesus accomplished our redemption by His sinless life, sacrificial death as our substitute, and physical resurrection from the dead, which proved that He was indeed God who had the authority to redeem us. In His resurrection He also defeated death forever. Jesus makes available to us the gift of eternal life—because Jesus Himself is Life. Again, all we must do to make that gift ours is recognize our sinfulness, repent, place our faith in His death on the cross as paying the death penalty we owe for that sin, and believe that God the Father raised Him from the dead.

Like the rest of the Bible, the Gospels are true. Where they speak of the same event yet do not seem to agree in exact detail, they actually complement each other, each writer filling in gaps in the accounts of the others. When one breaks off the story, another picks it up. The four independent historical narratives together produce a complete picture the way individual brush strokes are placed on the canvas by the artist to produce a painting that is more than just the sum of those colorful marks. Rather than being a source of confusion and doubt due to alleged human error, the supposed differences in the accounts of the eyewitnesses fit together to complete the story of the most significant events in world history: the events surrounding the beginning and the end of the first coming of the Lord Jesus, the Messiah. Matthew, Mark, Luke, and John, by the inspiration of the Holy Spirit, give us the entire story of God's plan of redemption from sin and death being fulfilled in one Man, Jesus of Nazareth, who was and is truly God, truly Man, Creator, and Savior. That plan was laid out and predicted in the Old Testament, making the entire Bible a consistent account of God's intervention throughout history to bring it to pass.

But you may be asking, "So what if all this is true? The world is falling apart around me. I've lost my job and maybe soon my house. How am I going to pay my bills and take care of my family? What does any of this stuff about the Bible and the Gospels being true have to do with the fact that my life has become chaos? What difference does being a Christian make in all this turmoil?"

Those are all valid questions as the whole world seems to be unraveling financially and socially in ways that have not been seen since the Great Depression of the 1920s and 30s. What difference does being a Christian really make? Philippians 4:6–7 answers that question and the others as well: "Be anxious for nothing, but in everything by prayer and supplication with thanksgiving let your requests be made known to God. And the peace of God, which surpasses all comprehension, will guard your hearts and your minds in Christ Jesus." Those verses are a command from God and a promise if the command is obeyed. We are not to worry about anything that life throws at us. Rather we are to pray, making requests for God to work out His will in our lives. But as we pray, we are also to give thanks, even for the difficulties. When we do that, God promises not necessarily to remove the problems but to guard our hearts from the unsettling effects of anxiety. Likewise, Romans 8:28 promises that everything that happens, good or bad, in the life of a Christian always works out to his or her benefit. But those promises are only for those who are believers in Jesus. Ultimately, however, the value of biblical Christianity doesn't lie in the fact that it "makes life work." Rather it lies in the fact that it is true.

Actually, the situation may be worse now than during the Great Depression because the cultural worldview of most Americans has changed dramatically in the past several decades.

I have talked with people who grew up in the 1930s during the Depression, and they told me that if a man came to their door asking to work for food, they had no fear that he meant them harm in any way. He simply was hungry and was willing to work to earn something to eat, so he worked and they fed him. That confidence is no longer warranted.

If the United States descends into a similar economic condition, I believe that, rather than asking to work for food, desperate people would more likely just take what they wanted. Another Great Depression would be a very dangerous time. What has happened in the last eight decades to bring about such a possible change in our response as a society? In my opinion, an underlying factor is that many in the church have for the most part abandoned their belief that the Bible is the inspired Word of God. I also believe that the primary reason for that is the widespread unbelief of a majority of Christian leaders in the first eleven chapters of Genesis as being historically accurate, leading to a perception that the Gospels also are not trustworthy.

Several ideas (such as the "gap" theory, the "day-age" theory, "progressive creation," etc.) have been proposed by Christian scholars and Bible teachers in the more than 150 years since Darwin published *The Origin of Species*. These ideas were developed to try to explain how the Big Bang, evolution, and billions of years of time could be added to Genesis 1–11 in order to make the historical accounts in the Bible conform to the stories promoted by atheistic scientists. However, these incorrect ideas about Genesis do not adequately explain the scientific evidence any better than does atheistic evolution. I believe that the result of these compromising notions being taught both in churches and in most Christian colleges and seminaries has been that a large number if not a majority of Christians have experienced just what I did. Their unbelief in the Genesis accounts of Creation and the Flood as true history and the lack of an explanation for the apparent inconsistencies between the Gospels have led to some degree of unbelief in the entire Bible.

Since Christian preachers and teachers could not (or worse, in an unsuccessful attempt to protect their standing in the eyes of agnostic or atheistic intellectuals, would not) defend Genesis as true, over time the entire Bible lost its reliability and authority as God's inerrant Word. The acceptance of these compromise positions by the majority of those in the church has raised a foundational question. If the first eleven chapters of Genesis are not true and there are mistakes in the Gospels, what parts of the Bible are true, and who decides what those parts are? As a consequence of the compromise, over the past century the dominant worldview of western society has gradually shifted from being based to varying degrees on belief in the God of the Bible toward atheism with its resulting drastic decline in morality and social order. Just watching the nightly news confirms that this decline is obvious everywhere in both public and private life.

But if the entire Bible is actually true, then what it says about both the past and the future must be seriously considered. Where are we in God's timeline of world events? What still lies ahead for believers as well as unbelievers? Just as Jesus' first coming was promised by God through the Old Testament prophets,[45] so is His

---
45 Numerous prophecies about Jesus' first coming are found in the Old Testament: the virgin birth of the Messiah in Isaiah 7:14, His birthplace of Bethlehem in

future return to the earth when, according to some conservative Bible teachers, He will rescue (rapture) the church out of what He refers to in Matthew 24:21 as a "great tribulation, such as has not occurred since the beginning of the world until now, nor ever will."[46] Ultimately God will destroy Satan and sin once and for all and will restore the heavens and earth to their original perfection where there will be no evil, no sin, no sickness, no death, and no sorrow (Isaiah 65:17–25, Revelation 21:1–22:5).

If you have never repented of your sins and received the undeserved free gift of eternal life, it is my prayer that you will do so now in order that you can both experience God's peace in the turbulence of this present life and enjoy Him and His renewed creation forever. If you have received that gift, it is also my hope that your faith has been strengthened by reading the combined narrative accounts of the miraculous beginning and end of Jesus' earthly life and His prediction of His Second Coming as the true history and prophecy that they are. As you read the complete Gospels now with the understanding that they are accurate, ask the Lord to show you that the entire Bible is God-breathed and can be read with the same confidence. I encourage you to read and reread it from Genesis to Revelation praying that God will reveal Himself as you do.

What is the significance of seeing that Genesis 1–11 is true

Micah 5:2, the date of His entry into Jerusalem as Israel's Prince in Daniel 9:24–26, His death as a substitute for our sins in Isaiah 53, and His resurrection from death in Psalm 16:10, 30:3, and others.

46 Matthew, Mark, and Luke as well as Daniel, Revelation, and others detail the order of events leading up to Jesus' return as conquering King for His church. A book entitled *The Sign* by Robert Van Kampen harmonizes the Old Testament and New Testament prophecies concerning Jesus' return and the end of the age.

history and that the four Gospels individually present one accurate historical account of Jesus' life, death, and resurrection from different perspectives? It has revolutionized my own perception of the entire Bible. I see it as the uncorrupted, historically as well as scientifically accurate and authoritative record of God's guidance of events to bring about His redemption of mankind from our sinful state. Rather than being full of errors and contradictions, as a spiritually blind, relativistic, and irrational world insists, God's Word is true!

CHAPTER 7

Consequences

It had been three months to the day since Kyle Jordan's trial. The whole thing had taken just under four hours. The jury of three men and nine women only stayed out in deliberation another four hours before returning with a guilty verdict. His court-appointed attorney had done a creditable job considering what he had to work with. But as Kyle had left an entire handprint on the counter top with his emphatic slap, it was hard to deny that he had been there. That plus the ballistics report on the bullet in the ceiling and the cumulative evidence of the eyewitnesses was more than enough to allow the jury to easily find him guilty.

At the moment he did not have a cellmate, so now here he sat, alone, on the edge of a bed that was not all that comfortable, staring at the dirty, once-white walls and the dark gray steel bars that marked the boundaries of this part of his new medium-security world. He could leave his cell for meals and exercise, of course. But there were other bars and walls and fences and above them guards with guns, all of which said in silent unison, "This far and that's it." It was a bleak life that faced him for the next seven to ten years, barring any extended period of good behavior that might get him out sooner.

Kyle had not made any new friends here. Not real friends anyway. Prison was not about building relationships; it was about surviving until you were released. That much he had learned quickly from the veterans of the system who had been in and out of jail several times already. "Just learn the routine, kid. Do what you're told and don't look nobody in the eye. It's the only way you'll make it." Kyle's new mentors had not been particularly encouraging.

In his deepening despair he found himself at times missing even the painful life he had had on the outside. At least then he had been free to go wherever he wanted. That is, as long as he didn't stray very far from the drug that set the unseen boundaries that defined his days. Kyle had been in prison for years without even knowing it. But occasionally his mind strayed to darker thoughts, and then the freedom he knew outside didn't seem worth the pain. At those times he found himself wishing he had not been caught so quickly. The last meth he had scored after the robbery had almost killed him, and on those dark days that were becoming more frequent, he wished it had. According to the arresting deputies, Kyle was in a coma when they found him lying on the ground beside his car.

It seems the moron who cooked the batch had been in a hurry. He had had to move his mobile lab that night and had cut the last step short just a little. As a result, some of the lethal ingredients had not been completely removed. If only the cops had been six hours later getting to him, he would have already started his adventure into oblivion. No more loneliness, no more pain. No more anything. At least that was what he had learned from his biology teacher in high school.

"You just live 'til you die, kid. Get used to it. You're nothing but an accident of nature—evolved pond slime. You're no more significant than any other animal." Kyle had believed him and, as a result, had lived like an animal, following his own instincts. No rules. Partying, drinking, smoking marijuana, doing meth, robbing a store, and finally winding up in prison. It seemed now that his whole meaningless life had been headed to this point.

Even the one brush with church he had as a young boy had not helped. He remembered the rather boring Sunday school teacher telling the sixth graders how the Gospels were not reliable sources of truth since they could not even agree on the historical details of some supposedly important events in Jesus' life. One Sunday morning his teacher had challenged the class of middle-school boys, "You don't believe there actually is such a place as hell do you?" Kyle was amazed that anybody could be so gullible as to believe that religion junk.

So here he was. Still alive, sort of, and not too thrilled at the prospect. The emptiness ate away at his insides. Little did he know that this new world he had entered was about to change. But, unlike the day in Willow Creek, this time he would not be the one to bring the change. The sound of footsteps stopping at his cell door roused Kyle from his black thoughts. There stood Frank, a big, muscular, not-very-friendly guard.

Had to have played offensive tackle sometime in a previous life, Kyle thought.

"Visitor, Jordan." Frank was a man of few words.

Kyle was confused. Nobody he knew would get within miles of a prison, let alone willingly go inside one. "You sure you got the right cell?"

"Yeah," Frank grunted. "You wanna see him or not? Don't matter to me."

"Yeah, I guess. Nothing else to do 'til supper." Kyle got up and stretched then walked the six feet to the door, putting his arms through the special gap in the bars to be handcuffed. Frank unlocked the door and slid it open with a clang, backing away so Kyle could step out. Their footsteps echoed down the long, cell-lined hallway as he walked silently in front of the massive guard toward the visiting room. All the while he was wracking his brain to figure out who it might be. It couldn't be a relative. As far as he knew no one in his family had even known where he was before the arrest. But an uncle had found him. When the robbery had been reported in the news, he had recognized Kyle and made some calls.

"In here." Frank opened the door to a sparse cubicle and stepped aside so Kyle could enter. The door with a large glass window shut behind him, and he sat in the single chair that faced the thick, wire-reinforced glass partition. On the other side were two empty chairs in a similar cubicle. Recessed microphones allowed for conversation. In a few minutes a man Kyle had never seen before sat down in one of the chairs. Late forties, early fifties. Medium height. Stocky. Pretty average guy. Kyle was getting good at sizing up people. The stranger gave Kyle a warm smile that sent lines radiating away from his eyes and mouth. He apparently smiled a lot. "Weird," Kyle thought.

"Hey, Kyle. My name's William Henderson, but you can call me Bill." Kyle made no response. Social graces are not widely practiced in prison. "You don't know me, but a relative of yours, an uncle, got in touch with my organization and asked if someone would visit you. He would have come himself, but he lives six hours away and can't drive that far right now because of a back problem. He is concerned about you and wanted me to see how you are doing."

"How am I doin'?" Kyle responded sarcastically, "What a stupid question. I'm in prison, that's how I'm doin'!"

"I know," Bill responded, his smile never dimming. "Prison is a hard place to get used to."

"And just how would you know that?" Kyle was not really curious. "You've never been on this side of the wall, man."

"Actually, I have," Bill replied quietly. "Not here, of course. I was in a prison upstate. Served six years of a ten-year sentence for armed robbery. Got out three years ago."

"Armed robbery, huh? What a coincidence. That's what I'm in for. So why do you come back to visit prisoners?" Kyle couldn't believe that once out of a place like this anyone would willingly set foot back inside regardless of the reason. "When I get outta here I ain't coming back to visit anybody. Nobody in here cares about me and I sure don't care about them!"

"You answered the question yourself," Bill smiled again. "I come to prisons to visit prisoners. That's what I do. Oh, by the way, you probably will come back. Most convicts do. I'd been in once before for burglary."

Kyle was not favorably impressed. Here was this rather average looking guy who had done some serious time and yet he comes to visit a total stranger in jail just because another stranger asks him to. He had to be nuts. "You really know how to make a guy feel all warm inside. You know you're crazy, don't you?" was all Kyle could say.

"No, not crazy, just changed is all. The kind of change that can keep you from coming back once you're out yourself." The big smile returned. "You see, about six months before my last release I met Jesus...."

"Whoa, dude! Stop right there," Kyle blurted out. "I don't care about no Jesus! I shoulda known this was about religion. I went to a church one time when I was a kid and that was enough. Go take your Jesus someplace where somebody gives a rip!" The look on Kyle's face was as cold as stone.

"I understand. I really do," the man replied quietly. "I felt the same way once. Listen, I'll go for now. I'll let your uncle know how you're doing." He got up and turned to leave but stopped. "Oh, I almost forgot. Your uncle is sending you some books I recommended. I found them interesting reading while I was inside. Maybe you will too. I'll be in touch, Kyle." With that and one last smile, the visitor was gone.

Days later Kyle was still intrigued by the visit. "Nice enough guy, but really weird," was all he would say to other inmates when they asked. Three weeks passed and the visit was all but forgotten when Frank appeared at Kyle's cell door.

"Jordan! Mail!" As always, short and to the point.

"Mail? For me?" Kyle got up from his bed. Trying to think what it might be, he remembered the books that were to be sent by his uncle. What was his name anyway? Jim? He couldn't recall. He thought he remembered his mother mentioning him before. Without a word he took the books that the guard handed through the bars and walked back to his bed.

"Let's see, *What is Scientific Creation?*, *The Bible and Science*, *Many Irrefutable Proofs*." Thumbing through the books showed that the prison staff had searched them for hidden contraband.

"Hmm," Kyle sneered. "Just what I thought—religion stuff." He tossed them in the trash can.

As the day wore on and he had nothing else to occupy his time, his mind drifted back to the books. He was tired from the three games of basketball in the yard and, since the whole cell block was now in lock-down due to a fight, TV was not an option at the moment. Boredom can make anything interesting, so in spite of himself Kyle got up and reached into the trash can, retrieving the gifts he had so ungratefully tossed.

"What can it hurt?" he said to no one and sat down and began reading.

Because of his earlier experience with chemistry, of sorts, the first book he opened was *The Bible and Science*. To say that he read with skepticism would be a serious understatement. He read with scorn. After all, his high school biology teacher had studied science and would not have even opened the cover. But he continued to read. Something would not let him put the book down. It seemed there was a lot of stuff about science in the Bible that he had never heard about. Of course, he had never actually read the Bible.

It took him a little more than a week to complete the first book. The author seemed to take the whole Bible seriously, even Genesis with the Creation and the Flood. The funny thing was that the guy was a scientist with a Ph.D.! His biology teacher had said that to be a real scientist you had to believe in evolution. But here was this real scientist who believed the Bible's account as if it were real history! Kyle didn't know what to think about this, so he just kept reading.

When Kyle finished the first book, there was no question he would finish them all. The scorn had given way gradually to curiosity. All three books had been written by scientists, and they all presented some pretty astounding information, even about the Bible's reliability as having no internal contradictions. To these obviously intelligent men, the Bible was completely trustworthy. If their claims were true, then Kyle had some thinking to do. These scientists refuted everything he had heard in school and had seen on television about millions of years of evolution. It couldn't really be true that the earth was only about six thousand years old! Could it?

Kyle had finally completed the three books. It had taken him almost a month. He was lying on his bunk one afternoon when Frank's rough call startled him.

"Jordan! Visitor!"

Bill! Kyle jumped to his feet. He had a list of questions a mile long and could not wait to have them answered. He waited in the cubicle, this time impatiently, for his visitor to arrive, his foot tapping a restless beat on the floor. By the time Mr. Henderson walked in, Kyle was so nervous that he stood up. As Kyle was about to speak he stopped short when another man whom he had never seen walked in right behind Mr. Henderson.

Henderson was the first to break the silence. "Kyle, this is your Uncle Jim."

Kyle did not know what to say, so all that came out was, "I was right! His name is Jim." Now rather embarrassed, he just looked at the strange man who had a vague resemblance to his mother.

"How do you do, Kyle." It was much too formal a greeting for a prison, but unlike Mr. Henderson, this man had never been inside a jail even to visit and was a bit uncomfortable. Jim put out his hand to shake then realized the glass was in the way. "Sorry," he said with a sheepish smile.

"It's okay," Kyle responded as they all sat down. "Nobody shakes hands in here even when there ain't any glass in the way. Besides, I'm cuffed anyway. Um, I'm glad you're feeling better, uh … Jim." The shock of meeting a long-lost relative, and in prison of all places, was awkward. "It's just strange meeting an uncle for the first time."

"I can imagine," Jim replied. "Actually, you have seen me before but you were very young. Six or seven I think. I'm your mother's older brother. Have you heard from her?"

"No, I haven't." A sad look crossed Kyle's face. He had not heard from his mother for years and for some reason he had not even thought about her since the day of the robbery. In spite of his hardness and the hardness of the place he was in, Kyle could feel tears begin to well up in his eyes as memories of her from long ago returned.

"She just took off a couple of years ago and we lost track of her. We've been trying to find her for a while." Jim fell silent as Mr. Henderson watched both of them.

"Kyle, have you read any of the books your uncle sent you?" Mr. Henderson asked after a few moments.

"Oh, yeah. Yeah!" Kyle suddenly remembered his anticipation. "I finished them a week or so ago. Thanks, Jim." Kyle was surprised by his own sincerity. "I can't remember the last time anybody gave me something for nothing." His excitement was evident in his voice. "I gotta tell you though, I almost threw them away when I saw what they were about. I've never been into religious stuff. But it's kind of cool that a scientist could believe the Creation and Flood story in the Bible. It makes you think." Kyle looked at Mr. Henderson.

"Yes, it does," Henderson replied, "but your uncle can tell you more about that than I can." Kyle looked back at Jim.

"That's right, Kyle. I'm a scientist myself. A biolochemist. I got my Ph.D. and have worked in the pharmaceutical industry for twenty-three years developing new drugs. I came out of college completely indoctrinated in evolution. And it almost destroyed me." Jim paused for effect.

"What do you mean?" Kyle asked.

"Well, I had been going to church since I married your Aunt Rebecca and was doing pretty well in my Bible study. I was even a deacon. But one Sunday while the preacher was talking about Jesus walking on the water I found myself wondering how it could have been done without a miracle. There had to be a natural explanation. People can't walk on water, you know. It slowly dawned on me that I really didn't believe the story." Jim was quiet for a moment, remembering the event. "As I sat there—in church, mind you—I came to the realization that I didn't really believe the Bible ... any of it! I'm a scientist. I couldn't believe in miracles, and the Bible is full of them. It hit me like a freight train."

Kyle was caught off guard by what he was hearing from this uncle whom he didn't really know. Ordinarily he would have left in a rage by now. He had always hated this kind of stuff. But, oddly, he really wanted to know what happened. Of course, it helped to remember that he was locked in his side of the visiting booth and couldn't leave anyway. "Go on Unc ..., uh ... Jim. What happened?"

"Well, Kyle, it was interesting. For some reason I didn't follow through with my first impulse to chuck the Bible and leave the church. Instead I did something I had never really done before. I prayed. I asked God to show me why I didn't believe in miracles, why I didn't believe the Bible." Jim was watching Kyle for visual hints of a wall going up in his mind. Seeing none, he went on.

"In a couple of weeks I began a new project at work dealing with a strain of bacteria that had developed a resistance to antibiotics. They are called 'super bugs' by people in my field. I had always thought of that phenomenon as proof of evolution, but a coworker told me that it wasn't that at all. He gave me an article about it written by a biologist who was a creationist. Here I was a Ph.D. and I never realized that natural bacteria populations have a small number of individuals mixed in that are already resistant to the antibiotics we use. All that happens is that the drugs kill off the non-resistant bacteria and leave the resistant ones. In a hospital environment where antibiotics are used all the time, with no competition from other non-resistant bacteria, the resistant ones survive and become dominant even though they would not thrive in 'the wild,' so to speak." Jim's voice showed his excitement. "The more I thought about it, the more it seemed to contradict evolution."

Kyle was obviously engrossed in his uncle's account. "Man, I've never heard any of this before."

"Neither have most other people, Kyle. It's just called 'evolution in action' by the media and we go on," Jim responded. "But what nobody says is that the resistance is due to a mutation that harms the bacteria slightly but not enough to kill them. It makes it harder for them to use nutrients they take in, or in some cases it becomes harder for the antibiotic to get inside the bacteria to begin with. They have lost genetic information and that has made them just a little less able to compete with the other bacteria outside of the sterile hospital. But while they are in the hospital they survive and multiply with no competition and no effective treatment, and they can still cause disease. Some are deadly. But evolution requires a gain of genetic information, not a loss." Jim paused as if for the final assault on the crumbling wall of doubt still remaining in Kyle's mind. Jim had this fleeting thought of Joshua about to blow his horn.

"I didn't quite know what to think, but I realized that drug resistance in bacteria was not an example of evolution the way I had always assumed. A few days later the same coworker gave me a book about creation science, one of the books I sent you." The more Jim talked, the more animated he became. Kyle was almost not even breathing as he listened. Mr. Henderson was silently praying.

Jim continued, "I could no longer reconcile what I was studying in the lab and had read in the article with what I had been taught about evolution, so I read the book. I was blown away, Kyle. That's the only way I can put it. All of a sudden I just knew that the information in the book and the article was correct. And you know, when I really thought about it, none of the research I was doing had anything to do with evolution. I just thought it did. One day it hit me, Kyle. Evolution is not real science at all! It can't even be tested one way or another! Real science is about proving theories by experimental testing, and no one, Kyle, no one, has ever been able to even think up an experiment to test evolution, let alone actually prove it. It simply is not science. It's philosophy, and bad philosophy at that. That revelation changed my life, Kyle. I just knew somehow that the Bible's account of how life got here had to be true."

Mr. Henderson could see that Kyle was more than just interested in what Jim was saying. It was as though he was drinking it up like a thirsty man in a desert drinks water when he stumbles upon an oasis. Kyle was astounded! Here was his own blood relative, a scientist, who believed the Bible! Kyle did not know what to say, so he said nothing. He had a sense that if he just kept listening, all of his questions would be answered without even having to ask them.

Jim continued, a smile crossing his face as he spoke. "The best was still ahead for me, Kyle, because some other doubts I had about the Bible were about to be answered as well. You see, I had believed that the New Testament, actually the entire Bible, was full of mistakes. The Gospel writers seemed to pretty much contradict each other in some areas. But I realized that if Genesis was true then maybe there would be an answer for my Gospel problem too. One day it occurred to me that it might be possible to put the different accounts together into a single narrative. At least portions of them seemed to dovetail together, mainly the parts about Jesus' birth and His death and resurrection. Maybe each was filling in the missing parts in the others to make a more complete account. When I put them together, the contradictions disappeared. The whole Bible is true, Kyle! But I didn't learn that; God revealed it to me. It had to be from God because not long before I wasn't really sure that I even wanted the Bible to be true!"

Kyle was amazed that his uncle had had the very same questions and objections about the Bible that he had had himself. All he could do was stare at this man who had walked into his life out of nowhere. Kyle had looked for "truth" in drugs and immorality of all sorts and had never found it, not really believing there was any such thing. And now here was this uncle giving him all the Truth he could handle. But he had a feeling there was more, so he waited for Jim to continue.

"But just believing in creation instead of evolution is not enough, Kyle. The book of Genesis is the foundation of the entire Bible. The Creation account underlies the one thing the Bible ultimately points to. I had realized years before that if Genesis is not true then the rest of the Bible may not be true either, even the part about how to go to heaven. And that … is the most important part. It's the main theme of the entire Bible. But suddenly I knew that it all was true. All that time, I had just been trying to be 'good enough' to get to heaven on my own, and nobody can do that." The tone of Jim's voice had gone from excitement to a quiet intensity. Kyle's eternity was in the balance, and Jim knew it.

Kyle listened carefully as his uncle and Mr. Henderson, taking turns, explained that Jesus, who was somehow God and Man, was the Creator of the universe and life. He listened as they explained that death entered the world as the result of the sin of the first man, Adam. He listened as they described how God judged the world's sin with a global Flood that killed all but those people and animals on the ark. He listened as they recounted how God confused the languages of Noah's descendants at Babel and scattered them over the earth. He listened, now totally focused on their words and the scripture they quoted, as they told how God eventually came to earth as a baby with the sole purpose of dying on a cross to pay for Kyle's own sins. He listened as they shared with him how he could know that he had eternal life by admitting he was a sinner, repenting of his sin, confessing that Jesus was God, and trusting in Jesus' death on the cross to pay the death penalty that Kyle owed for his sins. He listened as they shared that Jesus was raised from the dead to prove He was God and defeat death and that He is returning one day to restore the creation to the original perfection it displayed before sin entered and damaged it so terribly.

Then Mr. Henderson and Jim listened and rejoiced silently as Kyle prayed, through the long pent-up tears of a young man who knew he was being rescued not just from sin and the death it demanded but from the hell on earth his life had been, to receive the free gift of eternal life and repent of the innumerable sins he had committed. It took a while for Kyle to regain his composure enough to say goodbye to the men who had so gently broken into his life and turned it thoroughly upside down, or rather right side up.

Kyle left the cubicle and walked quietly, and for the first time in his life joyfully, in front of Frank back to his cell. But how could that be? He was still in prison. As they passed cells full of men just as hopeless and empty as he had so recently been himself, Kyle's heart broke for them and the tears started all over again. It was a good thing Frank could not see him crying. Or was it? Kyle did not really know how to deal with the emotions flowing through the depths of his soul at the moment. In the coming days he would let God sort them out as he began to think about how he would share his new freedom with the men around him. He couldn't wait to get the Bible Jim was going to send so he could read it cover to cover and then start again.

As Kyle approached his cell, he realized that he no longer felt the hostility toward the guard that he had before ... before what? Before this new life that was now full of purpose and promise had been given to him by Jesus. He somehow knew that, even though Frank was not an inmate himself, he was just as much a prisoner as Kyle had been before coming here. He now wanted more than anything to be able to tell Frank about what he had just experienced, but for now he would just pray for the big, tough guard. Little did he know that Frank would soon begin to see a profound difference in Kyle and would ask about it himself.

As he stepped into his cell, Kyle thought about the four people back in Willow Creek that he had so terrified. He wanted to go back to apologize and let them see that Jesus had changed him. He wanted to make up somehow for all the pain he had caused.

The door slammed shut behind Kyle. He looked around the cramped living space that he had so recently left that would continue to be his home for quite a while. But it was okay. It looked different than it had such a short time earlier. It was still dirty but cleaner somehow, less dark. He stepped to the narrow, barred, second story window that looked out over the walled exercise yard and beyond. He gazed at the trees and rolling landscape that he could always see in the distance beyond the wall, less clearly now through the summer afternoon haze. They were the same trees that, an hour earlier, had mocked him by their mere existence, reminding him that they were outside and he was not. But that was okay too.

He smiled, something he had not done in a long time, because he knew that the God who had created all trees and put those particular ones there for him to see, the God who had kept him alive when he had wanted to die and nearly had, the God who had been chasing him for so long, had finally caught him and taken him prisoner. It would be a while before the irony of that truth would hit him. And that would be more than okay. The raging anger and emptiness was now full of a quiet peace and joy that would astound Kyle for the rest of his life. He knew that for the first time in his life, here behind bars, he was no longer really in prison.

"How was it Jim had described me after I prayed?" Kyle asked himself out loud. "Oh yeah, I'm a new creation in Christ."

As the reality of that truth settled into Kyle's heart, it struck him that the bars and walls, the guards and guns that he had hated just an hour or so ago didn't matter anymore. Nothing mattered but Jesus and sharing Him with the men around him while he was in prison. He also knew that after he got out he would come back. But he wouldn't come back because he couldn't stay clean. He wouldn't come back because he couldn't make it on the outside. Like Bill, he would come back to this prison and would go to any other prison he could get into to visit the men inside to talk to them, to build relationships with them. He would come back so God could use him to draw them out of the dark into the Light and out of death into Life and set them free.

Appendix

Websites of interest for further Bible apologetics/creation/evangelistic resources:

Christian Answers Network
Web address: *www.christiananswers.net*

Website content: General questions answered about the Bible and historical, biblical Christian doctrine on a wide range of topics

Christian Ministries International
Web address: *www.creation.com*

Website content: Generally popular-level biblical creation information from a scientific and theological basis

Institute for Creation Research
Web address: *www.icr.org*

Website content: Biblical creation information from a scientific and theological basis—more semi-technical to technical content

Zion's Hope Ministries
Web address: *www.zionshope.org*

Website content: Biblical Christian doctrine focusing on Israel and the Middle East

Works Cited

"Battle for Science's Soul." *Creation the Journal of the Creation Science Movement*. Creation Science Movement, Sept. 2005. Web. <https://www.csm.org.uk/journals/2005-4.pdf?PHPSESSID=donjmkalr>.

Catchpoole, David. "Surtsey Still Surprises." *Creation* 30.1 (2007): 32-34. Creation Ministries International. Web. Apr. 2009. <http://creation.com/surtsey-still-surprises>.

DeYoung, Donald. *Thousands...not Billions Tearing Down an Icon of Evolution*. New Leaf Pr, 2005. Print.

Grigg, Russell. "Darwin's Arguments Against God, How Darwin Rejected the Doctrines of Christianity." *Creation.com*. Creation Ministries International, 13 June 2008. Web. 4 Sept. 2008. <http://creationontheweb.com/content/view/5703>.

"Idaho Scientists for Quality Science Education | NCSE." *NCSE | National Center for Science Education - Defending the Teaching of*

Evolution in Public Schools. 2000. Web. 24 Jan. 2009. <http://ncse.com/media/voices/idaho-scientists-quality-science-education>.

Lamont, Ann. *21 Great Scientists Who Believed the Bible.* Brisbane, Australia: Creation Science Foundation, 1995. Print.

Matthews, L. H. *Origin of Species.* London: J. M. Dent & Sons, 1971. Print.

"Penn State Live - Deep Sea Rocks Point to Early Oxygen on Earth." *Penn State Live - The University's Official News Source.* Web. 1 Sept. 2009. <http://live.psu.edu:80/story/38514>.

Sarfati, Jonathan. "15 Loopholes in the Evolutionary Theory of the Origin of Life: Summary." Creation Ministries International. Web. 2008. <http://creation.com/loopholes-in-the-evolutionary-theory-of-the-origin-of-life-summary>.

Sarfati, Jonathan. "Electric DNA." *Creation* 29.2 (2007): 40-41. Creation Ministries International. Web. 24 Jan. 2009. <http://creation.com/electric-dna>.

Sarfati, Jonathan. "Knowing Toil, Knowing Soil." *Creation* 28.3 (2006): 33-35. Creation Ministries International. Web. 2008. <http://creation.com/knowing-toil-knowing-soil>.

Sarfati, Jonathan. "The Yellowstone Petrified Forest: Evidence of Catastrophy." *Creation* 21.2 (1999): 25. Creation Ministries

International. Web. May 2009. <http://creation.com/the-yellowstone-petrified-forests>.

Snelling, Andrew A. *Earth's Catastrophic Past: Geology, Creation, & the Flood.* Vol. 1. Dallas, TX: Institute for Creation Research, 2009. Print.

Snelling, Andrew A. *Earth's Catastrophic Past: Geology, Creation, & the Flood.* Vol. 2. Dallas, TX: Institute for Creation Research, 2009. Print.

Snelling, Andrew A. "Sedimentation Experiments: Nature Finally Catches Up." *Creation* 11.2 (1997): 125-26. Creation Ministries International. Web. May 2009. <http://creation.com/sedimentation-experiments-nature-finally-catches-up>.

Snelling, Andrew A. "The Case of the 'Missing' Geologic Time." *Creation* 14.3 (1992): 30-35. Creation Ministries International. Web. 2008. <http://creation.com/the-case-of-the-missing-geologic-time>.

Swenson, Keith. "More and More Wrong Dates: Radio-dating in Rubble." *Creation* 23.3 (2001): 23-25. Creation Ministries International. Web. 2007. <http://creation.com/more-and-more-wrong-dates-radio-dating-in-rubble>.

Van Kampen, Robert. *The Sign.* Wheaton, IL: Crossway, 2000. Print

Walker, Tas. "Mud Experiments Overturn Long-held Geological Beliefs." Creation Ministries International, 9 Jan. 2008. Web. 24

Jan. 2009. <http://creation.com/mud-experiments-overturn-long-held-geological-beliefs>.

"Was Jesus Born in a Stable? - ChristianAnswers.Net." *Christian Answers® Network™ (ChristianAnswers.Net): Multilingual Answers, Reviews, Ministry Resources, and More! [Home].* Associates for Biblical Research. Web. Aug. 2000. <http://christiananswers.net/q-abr/abr-a012.html>.

Weinberger, Lael. "Assumptions, Presumptions and the Future of Faith." *Journal of Creation* 22.2 (2008): 25. Print.

Wieland, Carl. "Surtsey, the Young Island That 'Looks Old'" *Creation* 17.2 (1995): 10-13. Creation Ministries International. Web. 2008. <http://creationontheweb.com/content/view/1745/>.

Wieland, Carl. "The Marvelous Message Molecule." *Creation* 17.4 (1995): 10-13. Print.

Wieland, Carl. "The Not-so-Nobel Decision." *Creation* 26.4 (2004): 40-42. Print.

Wilson, Bill, comp. *A Ready Defense: The Best of Josh McDowell.* Nashville, TN: Thomas Nelson, 1993. Print.

For more information about Everett Coates and his book *Why The Gospel Witnesses Agree,* please visit:

www.gospelwitnesses.com